Invention, Innovation and U.S. Federal Laboratories

For Carol

Invention, Innovation and U.S. Federal Laboratories

Albert N. Link

Virginia Batte Phillips Distinguished Professor of Economics, University of North Carolina at Greensboro, USA

Edward Elgar
PUBLISHING

Cheltenham, UK • Northampton, MA, USA

Published by
Edward Elgar Publishing Limited
The Lypiatts
15 Lansdown Road
Cheltenham
Glos GL50 2JA
UK

Edward Elgar Publishing, Inc.
William Pratt House
9 Dewey Court
Northampton
Massachusetts 01060
USA

A catalogue record for this book
is available from the British Library

Library of Congress Control Number: 2020944683

This book is available electronically in the **Elgar**online
Business subject collection
http://dx.doi.org/10.4337/9781800370029

ISBN 978 1 80037 001 2 (cased)
ISBN 978 1 80037 002 9 (eBook)
Printed and bound by CPI Group (UK) Ltd, Croydon, CR0 4YY

Contents

About the author

Albert N. Link, Ph.D. is the Virginia Batte Phillips Distinguished Professor at the University of North Carolina at Greensboro (UNCG). He received the B.S. degree in mathematics from the University of Richmond (Phi Beta Kappa) and the Ph.D. degree in economics from Tulane University. After receiving the Ph.D., he joined the economics faculty at Auburn University, was later Scholar-in-Residence at Syracuse University, and then he joined the economics faculty at UNCG in 1982. In 2019, Link was awarded the title and honorary position of Visiting Professor at the University of Northumbria, UK.

Professor Link's research focuses on entrepreneurship, technology and innovation policy, the economics of R&D, and policy/program evaluation. He is currently the Editor-in-Chief of the *Journal of Technology Transfer*. He is also co-editor of *Foundations and Trends in Entrepreneurship* and founder/editor of *Annals of Science and Technology Policy*.

Among his more than 60 books, some of the more recent ones are: *Technology Transfer and US Public Sector Innovation* (Edward Elgar, 2020), *Collaborative Research in the United States: Policies and Institutions for Cooperation among Firms* (Routledge, 2020), *Sources of Knowledge and Entrepreneurial Behavior* (University of Toronto Press, 2019), *Handbook for University Technology Transfer* (University of Chicago Press, 2015), *Public Sector Entrepreneurship: U.S. Technology and Innovation Policy* (Oxford University Press, 2015), *Bending the Arc of Innovation: Public Support of R&D in Small, Entrepreneurial Firms* (Palgrave Macmillan, 2013), *Valuing an Entrepreneurial Enterprise* (Oxford University Press, 2012), *Public Goods, Public Gains: Calculating the Social Benefits of Public R&D* (Oxford University Press, 2011), *Employment Growth from Public Support of Innovation in Small Firms* (W.E. Upjohn Institute for Employment Research, 2011), and *Government as Entrepreneur* (Oxford University Press, 2009).

Professor Link's other research consists of more than 200 peer-reviewed journal articles and book chapters, as well as numerous government reports. His scholarship has appeared in such journals as the *American Economic Review*, the *Journal of Political Economy*, the *Review of Economics and Statistics*, *Economica*, *Research Policy*, *Economics of Innovation and New Technology*, the *European Economic Review*, *Small Business Economics*, *ISSUES in Science and Technology*, *Scientometrics*, and the *Journal of Technology Transfer*.

Professor Link's public service includes being a member of the National Research Council's research team that conducted the 2010 evaluation of the U.S. Small Business Innovation Research (SBIR) program. Based on that assignment, he later testified before Congress in April 2011 on the economic benefits associated with the SBIR program. Link also served from 2007 to 2012 as the U.S. Representative to the United Nations (Geneva) in the capacity of co-vice chairperson of the Team of Specialists on Innovation and Competitiveness Policies Initiative for the Economic Commission for Europe. In October 2018, Link delivered the European Distinguished Scholar Lecture at the Commission's Joint Research Centre (Seville).

Acknowledgements

The content and structure of this book have benefitted greatly from comments and suggestions from my colleagues in the Department of Economics at the University of North Carolina at Greensboro, Eric Howard and Martijn van Hasselt; and from my virtual colleague at Dartmouth College, John Scott. I am grateful to all for their guidance and support. Of course, any remaining shortcomings are my own.

Abbreviations

$2019	Year 2019 constant dollars
AUTM	Association of University Technology Managers
BLS	Bureau of Labor Statistics
CAP	Cross Agency Priority
C.F.R.	Code of Federal Regulations
CRADA	Cooperative Research and Development Agreement
DHS	Department of Homeland Security
DOC	Department of Commerce
DOD	Department of Defense
DOE	Department of Energy
DOI	Department of Interior
DOT	Department of Transportation
EPA	Environmental Protection Agency
FLC	Federal Laboratory Consortium
FY	Fiscal Year
GAO	Government Accounting Office
HC	Human capital
HHS	Health and Human Services
ICT	Information and Communication Technology
Kn	Stock of knowledge
L	Number of employees
MFP	Multifactor Productivity
NASA	National Aeronautics and Space Administration
NBS	National Bureau of Standards
NIST	National Institute of Standards and Technology
OLS	Ordinary Least Squares
OSTP	Office of Science and Technology Policy

PMA	President's Management Agenda
R&D	Research and Development
RD	R&D
ROI	Return on Investment
STEM	Science, Technology, Engineering, and Mathematics
TC	Technical capital
TFP	Total Factor Productivity
TTO	Technology Transfer Office
USDA	U.S. Department of Agriculture
USPTO	U.S. Patent and Trademark Office
VA	Department of Veterans Affairs

1. The genesis of inventive ideas

SETTING THE STAGE

The title of a book says much about the content of a book. This book is clearly about inventions, and the genesis of the specific inventions that I will discuss have taken place in U.S. federal laboratories.[1] To be more specific, the inventions that I discuss in this book are defined by the technology transfer mechanism known by the term "invention disclosures"—a term of art/science that I will define and discuss below—that refers to an aspect of the tangible results from inventive ideas in a federal laboratory.

However, there is more to this book than simply a heuristic and descriptive analysis of invention disclosures in U.S. federal laboratories. This book also represents an open call, and perhaps even a first step, toward understanding the genesis of the process of the transfer of new technology developed in federal laboratories to organizations in both the public and private sectors.

The overarching theme of this book aside for the moment, I realize that I am being a bit presumptuous in this opening chapter in my effort to identify, as the title of this chapter suggests, the genesis of inventive ideas. And perhaps my presumptuousness is exaggerated by the fact that I offer below thoughts about the genesis of ideas, be they good ideas or even bad ideas. I am focusing on ideas per se. I urge the reader to keep in mind that my intent for this chapter is to set the stage, or to provide a foundation or platform, for the arguments and analyses that follow in this book.

Context is always important, and the context or backdrop for thinking about the genesis of inventive ideas might be traced in the modern literature to the concept of a knowledge production function (although I make an effort below to trace the genesis of ideas further back in the history of thought). Within the discipline of economics, a starting point for a discussion about a knowledge production function—not of knowledge per se—arguably begins with how researchers have interpreted a footnote in Zvi Griliches's seminal journal article, "Issues in Assessing the Contribution of Research and Development to Productivity Growth" (Griliches, 1979).

Griliches's objective in his 1979 article was, in part, to discuss the form a production function used to describe the current level of technological knowledge observed in an economic unit (i.e., in a firm, a laboratory, a university, or even a country) at a specific point in time. He posited in his article that the current level of technological knowledge is functionally related to current and past levels of research and development (R&D) expenditures in that unit. He referred to this relationship in his footnote as a knowledge production function.

Over the past four decades, a rich and creative literature has developed in the field of economics.[2] One framework to motivate a discussion about the determinants of the production of knowledge is based on the following conceptual model. At a given point in time, let *Kn* represent the existing stock of knowledge. Let *HC* represent the available level of human capital, and let *TC* represent the available level of technical capital. Thus, one might write:

$$Kn = F \, (HC, \, TC) \qquad\qquad (1.1)$$

Academic researchers who have estimated empirically variants of a model like the one in equation (1.1) within the context of a technology-based economic unit—generally within a private sector technology-based firm (e.g., Hall and Ziedonis, 2001; Czarnitzki, Kraft, and Thorwarth, 2009), but not always (e.g., Link, 2019; Link and Van Hasselt, 2019; Link and Oliver, 2020)—have approximated *Kn* in terms of a count of new patent applications.

The use of new patent applications (*Patent Applications*) as the metric to approximate the stock of knowledge, that is, technical knowledge in terms of the literature just referenced, was perhaps (*likely* might be a more accurate word than *perhaps*) driven by the availability of data to proxy new knowledge.[3] However, there might be an alternative and perhaps more accurate approach to the measurement of *Kn* in a technology-based economic unit, and that approach could involve quantifying the existing stock of inventive ideas.

What I have in mind is that the stock of inventive ideas (*Inventive Ideas*), which I will define below in terms of invention disclosures as suggested above, is related to the available stock of *HC* and *TC* as:

$$Inventive\ Ideas = f \, (HC, \, TC) \qquad\qquad (1.2)$$

where the functional form of $f\,(\cdot)$ in equation (1.2) is not necessarily the same as $F\,(\cdot)$ in equation (1.1) just above. Then, it is *Inventive Ideas* from equation (1.2), in the context of the extant literature, that become related to *Patent Applications* as:

$$Patent\ Applications = G \, (Inventive\ Ideas) \qquad\qquad (1.3)$$

where the function for $G\,(\cdot)$ is not necessarily the same as either $f\,(\cdot)$ or $F\,(\cdot)$ presented in the previous two equations.

Quite reasonably, a perceptive reader might say: "What's the big deal! All that has been shown in these three equations is that an intermediate step has been added to an already defined body of research." That perceptive reader would be correct ... absolutely correct. But, in my view, the intermediate step being referred to is an important step, and it is one that has been overlooked, to the best of my knowledge, in the relevant literature. From a conceptual, and perhaps from a theoretical level as well, this intermediate step emphasizes, as I discuss below, that the omnipresent human capital variable (HC) is an important policy target variable along with, of course, technical capital (TC).

EXPERIENCES → INVENTIVE IDEAS

As a starting point for my endeavor to think about inventive ideas, I begin with insight of John Locke as presented in his famous treatise, *An Essay Concerning Human Understanding*, first published in 1690.[4]

Locke emphasized that any and all ideas emanate from sensation or reflection. He wrote (Locke, 1690 [1996], p. 33):

> Every man being conscious to himself, that he thinks, and that which his mind is employed about whilst thinking being the *ideas*, that are there, 'tis past doubt, that men have in their minds several *ideas* ... *All ideas come from sensation or reflection.*

With regard to "sensation or reflection," Locke went on to emphasize in his *Essay* that perceptions are a foundational building block of one's ideas (1690 [1996], pp. 33–4):

> *[O]ur senses*, conversant about particular sensible objects, do *convey into the mind* several distinct *perceptions* of things, according to those various ways, wherein those objects do affect them: and thus we come by those *ideas* we have of *yellow, white, heat, cold, soft, hard, bitter, sweet,* and all those which we call sensible qualities, which when I say the senses convey into the mind, I mean, they from external objects convey into the mind what produces there those *perceptions*. This great source, of most of the *ideas* we have, depending wholly upon our senses, and derived by them to the understanding, I call *SENSATION.*

And Locke went even further to say (1690 [1996], p. 34):

> [The] source of *ideas*, every man has wholly in himself: and though it be not sense, as having nothing to do with external objects; yet it is very like it, and might properly enough be called internal sense. But as I call the other *sensation*, so I call this *REFLECTION*, the *ideas* it affords being such only, as the mind gets by reflecting on its own operations within itself.

Perhaps a more eloquent summary of Locke's view about experiences, and that is anticipatory of the theme of this book, is offered in the following paragraph in *Essay* (Locke, 1690 [1996], p. 33):

> Let us then suppose the mind to be, as we say, white paper, void of all characters, without any *ideas*; how comes it to be furnished? Whence comes it by that vast store, which the busy and boundless fancy of man has painted on it, with an almost endless variety? Whence has it all the materials of reason and knowledge? To this I answer, in one word, from *experience*; in that, all our knowledge is founded; and from that it ultimately derives itself. Our observation employed either, about *external sensible objects* [i.e., sensations], *or about the internal operations of our minds, perceived and reflected on by ourselves* [i.e., reflection], *is that, which supplies our understandings with all the materials of thinking*. These two are the fountains of knowledge, from whence all the *ideas* we have, or can naturally have, do spring.

Centuries later, it was Albert Einstein who is quoted to have said: "The only source of knowledge is experience."[5]

Reflecting on Locke's thoughts does raise several questions, three of which are:

- Do more experiences lead to more ideas?
- Do more experiences lead to better ideas?
- Must an idea be acted on before judgment is rendered about where that idea lies on a good idea to bad idea spectrum?

Alfred Nobel is quoted to have said: "If I have a thousand ideas and only one turns out to be good, I am satisfied."[6] And, anticipating that many of the readers of this book will have an academic background, I am usurping three additional questions:

- How does one measure experiences?
- How does one measure ideas, inventive ideas in particular?
- Can one quantify a relationship of the form: *Experiences* → *Inventive Ideas*?[7]

Theodore Schultz, recipient of the Nobel Memorial Prize in Economic Sciences in 1979, argued that if experiences influence one's abilities, then the economic value of one's experiences is related, at least in some part, to one's educational background (Schultz, 1975). Building on this perspective, Fritz Machlup later wrote that formal education is only one source of knowledge; knowledge is also gained experientially and at different rates by different individuals. Individuals can accrue knowledge from their day to day experiences, which "will normally induce reflection, interpretations, discoveries, and generalization ..." (Machlup, 1980, p. 179).

Steven Johnson, the author of the *New York Times* bestseller *Where Good Ideas Come From*, set forth the following related point of view (2010, pp. 35–6):

> Good ideas are not conjured out of thin air; they are built out of a collection of existing parts, the composition of which expands (and, occasionally, contracts) over time … [T]he history of cultural progress is, almost without exception, a story of one door leading to another door, exploring the palace one room at a time.

Building, figuratively as well as literally, on Johnson's door to door metaphor, I reflect on a fact that I learned about from reading Jon Gertner's *New York Times* bestseller, *The Idea Factory: Bell Labs and the Great Age of American Innovation*. In the early 1930s, Bell Labs began to build a new research facility in Murray Hill, New Jersey, in an effort to remove itself from the hustle and bustle of New York city life. Among other things, the Murray Hill Bell Labs facility was intentionally designed to be constructed in a manner that would encourage an interchange of ideas among colleagues (2012, p. 77):

> By intention, everyone would be in one another's way. Members of the technical staff would often have both laboratories and small offices—but these might be in different corridors, therefore making it necessary to walk between the two, and all but assuring a chance encounter or two with a colleague during the commute. By the same token, the long corridor of the wing that would house many of the physics researchers was intentionally made to be seven hundred feet in length. It was so long that to look down it from one end was to see the other end disappear at a vanishing point. Traveling its length without encountering a number of acquaintances, problems, diversion, and ideas would be almost impossible. Then again, that was the point. Walking down that impossibly long tiled corridor, a scientist on his [or her] way to lunch in the Murray Hill cafeteria was like a magnet rolling past iron filings [in the doors of colleagues].

Perhaps, then, a proxy for one's potential set of experiences that influence one's inventive ideas might be one's vocational and intellectual network, that is, the number of one's vocational and intellectual colleagues. This is certainly not a perfect proxy for one's set of experiences, and some readers might go further and say that this is not even a second or third best proxy. I offer no defense for it being perfect or even second best, I simply offer it, without excuse, for consideration. One of the many reasons for the imperfectness of my suggested proxy is that an individual's set of experiences predates one being active in the pursuit of one's vocation. Also, living in an information accessible environment—the information and communications technology (ICT) age as it is often called—offers an individual, regardless of one's demographics, the opportunity to gain experiences from others who might, literally speaking, not happen to be along a tiled corridor that leads to the lunch cafeteria.[8,9]

Referring back to the point above about the importance of face to face interchanges, consider the conceptual argument about experiences that has long been offered for, as an example, the establishment and ongoing operations of university science and technology parks such as Stanford Research Park in California, founded in 1951; Cornell Business and Technology Park in New York, founded in 1952; Research Triangle Park in North Carolina, founded in 1959; and the list goes on. The initial argument for the construction of such parks, and for the allocation of resources for their growth and development—and there are many more park examples to support this claim as I, along with my co-author John Scott, have documented through our own research and writings (Link and Scott, 2003, 2006, 2007, 2012, 2013)—was that there are spillover benefits from scientists and researchers being physically close to one another. The argument is simple: tacit knowledge is more easily exchanged when scientists are in close proximity to one another.

More to this point, John Scott and I have previously pointed out (e.g., Link and Scott, 2018; Link, 2020) that there are other arguments in support of the juxtaposition of a science and technology park's scientists and researchers to one another as well as to a university's scientists and researchers, and these arguments follow directly from economic theory. These arguments, summarized below, relate to the agglomeration benefits and the sharing of knowledge that results from being in contact in a face to face manner.[10]

Alfred Marshall (1919) made the point, as I and others have interpreted it, that there are competitive benefits stemming from cooperation among industrial firms that are geographically close to each other. The science and technology park concept of sharing knowledge, often specialized knowledge among research-oriented firms, as well as with their host university, through proximity brings about the competitive benefits associated with ideas and even new research directions. Specifically, Marshall (1919, p. 599) wrote:

> The broadest and in some respects most efficient forms of cooperation are seen in a great industrial district where numerous specialized branches of industry have been welded almost automatically into an organic whole.

Also, cluster theory, as interpreted by for example Paul Westhead and Stephen Batstone (1998), predicts that the process of creating innovations is more efficient because of experiential knowledge spillovers, enhanced benefits, and lower costs that result from the clusters of research and technology-based firms being near a university. Barriers to tacit knowledge, search costs, and acquisition costs are all reduced when economic units participate with one another in a cluster-like environment. In other words, clustering engenders a two-way or reciprocal flow of scientific knowledge. As a result, it is perhaps not surprising that, as I along with John Scott (e.g., Link and Scott, 2003) found from our survey-based research of university provosts, universities are able to attribute more publications and patents, greater success getting extramural funding, improved placement of doctoral graduates, and an enhanced ability to hire preeminent scholars to having a science and technology park physically located on their campuses (if not on their campuses, then very close by).

In addition to the benefits of firms clustering together within a park, the issue of the proximity of a park to its university, that is, the clustering of firm scientists and researchers with university scientists and researchers, might also influence the success of the park. Kelsi Hobbs, John Scott, and I, through our empirical endeavors (Link and Scott, 2006; Hobbs, Link, and Scott, 2017a, 2017b), have shown that the growth of employees over time in university science and technology parks increases the more closely the park is located to the university campus. This empirical finding should perhaps not be an unexpected one given the arguments I have summarized just above.

The list of agglomeration examples goes on. As David Audretsch (1998, p. 21) noted, although not with respect to science and technology parks: "[Tacit] knowledge … is best transmitted via face to face interaction and through frequent and repeated contact." And along those same lines of thought, Edward Glaeser and colleagues (1992, p. 1126) pointed out, although also not with respect to science and technology parks: "Intellectual breakthroughs must cross hallways and streets more easily than oceans and continents."

Referring again to the relationship between employment growth and proximity of a science and technology park to its host university, the relationship ceases to be observed in the data beginning with the new millennium (year 2000) during which time the ICT revolution is said to have begun and then rapidly accelerated.[11] Simply, face to face interactions could and did occur electronically and at a much lower cost than physical face to face interactions. As Kelsi Hobbs, John Scott, and I wrote (2017a, p. 503): "[T]he ICT revolution mitigated aspects of the need for scientists to have face to face interactions with university scientists …" Even after the ICT revolution began and its effects were part of everyday life, it is still experiences gained, although using a technology-based medium of exchange, that matter for the development of and nurturing of creative ideas.

Finally, path dependency theory, as embraced through the scholarship of for example Paul David (1985), predicts that for technologies spawned by ideas generated in a university, creating a science and technology park (from the perspective of the university) and locating in the park (from the perspective of firms) give positive reinforcing feedback to both parties to continue their particular scientific development paths for the development of a particular technology. A university's science and technology park can be said to reinforce path dependence that locks in the success for the technology developed in the park that relies on the ideas of university scientists and researchers (Link and Scott, 2018).

Thus, the foundation for the following chapters in this book is that the genesis of inventive ideas is related to one's experiences, and one's experiences are richer when (1) interacting among as well as conducting research among groups of colleagues rather than in isolation, and when (2) having appropriate complementary resources.[12] This relationship network forms the basis of the arguments and analyses that are presented in the chapters in the rest of this book under the rubric of what I am calling the *Experiences → Inventive Ideas* paradigm.

THE CHAPTERS THAT FOLLOW

The remainder of this book is outlined as follows. In Chapter 2, I define what I mean by the term *Inventive Ideas*. That is, I define *Inventive Ideas* to be reflected in, and thus measured in terms of, the number of new invention disclosures in a federal laboratory. While the invention disclosures that I study below are those that originate from scientists and researchers in federal laboratories, the concept of invention disclosures nevertheless goes beyond the boundaries of a federal laboratory as I will discuss below. In part, my focus on federal laboratories is not only driven by data availability, as I stated in an endnote to this chapter, but also it is driven by a conspicuous void of empirical research on elements of technology transfer in federal laboratories (although published research efforts by John Scott and me, as well as others, are slowly beginning to fill that void).[13]

Federal laboratories have long been an important technology-based infrastructure, as well as an institutional platform, in the United States. For example, the development of the Manhattan Project[14] at the Los Alamos National Laboratory[15] is no doubt remembered by many around the world. Jumping ahead in time, President Jimmy Carter—in his October 1979 address to the U.S. Senate Committee on Commerce, Science, and Transportation and the Select Committee on Small Business; and to the U.S. House of Representatives Committee on Science and Technology and the Committee on Small Business—set forth a number of policy initiatives to address the productivity slowdown that was plaguing the U.S. economy during the time period of the 1970s (and the productivity slowdown will be discussed in Chapter 2).[16] In President Carter's address, he pointed out the importance of "the transfer of knowledge from Federal laboratories" (Carter, 1979, p. 64) for helping to "ensure our country's continued role as the world leader in industrial innovation" (p. 63).

Technology transfer from federal laboratories was also emphasized in *U.S. Technology Policy*, issued by President George H.W. Bush in 1990 (Executive Office of the President, 1990, pp. 1–6):

> Government policies can help establish a favorable environment for private industry [by improving] the transfer of Federal laboratories' R&D results to the private sector [and by expediting] the diffusion of the results of Federally-conducted R&D to industry, including licensing of inventions ...

Federal laboratories were more recently highlighted, in terms of the national importance of technology transfer, by President Barack Obama. In his October 2011 Presidential Memorandum—Accelerating Technology Transfer and Commercialization of Federal Research in Support of High-Growth Businesses—President Obama wrote (Obama, 2011):[17]

> Innovation fuels economic growth, the creation of new industries, companies, jobs, products and services, and the global competitiveness of U.S. industries. One driver of successful innovation is technology transfer, in which the private sector adapts Federal research for use in the marketplace . . . I direct that [Federal laboratories] establish goals and measure performance, streamline administrative processes, and facilitate local and regional partnerships in order to accelerate technology transfer and support private sector commercialization.

President Donald Trump, in his *The President's Management Agenda* (Trump, undated, p. 47), set forth the goal to: "Improve the transfer of technology from federally funded research and development to the private sector to promote U.S. economic growth and national security" for modernizing government for the 21st century.[18] Specifically, he wrote (p. 47):

> For America to maintain its position as the leader in global innovation, bring products to market more quickly, grow the economy, and maintain a strong national security innovation base, it is essential to optimize technology transfer and support programs to increase the return on investment (ROI) from federally funded R&D.

In Chapter 2, I will also describe trends over time in invention disclosures, aggregated from federal laboratories to the agency level. These trends, across federal agencies, show that invention disclosures have not been increasing over time, and in fact in several agencies they have even been decreasing. If new inventive ideas do not increase over time, might the relevance of scientific ideas that ultimately stem from public investments in scientific and technical research in federal laboratories stagnate? I will revisit this question a number of times throughout this book. In my view, the decline in the number of invention disclosures, or the non-increase in invention disclosures, is worrisome because it signals a decline in new scientific ideas. And, based on what I have written above, many writers think that ideas beget ideas.

More to the point, we know from the scholarly writings of James Burke (1978) that inventions are linked. And inventions are the product of inventive ideas. If the growth of inventive ideas stagnates, from where will future inventions come? If the growth of future inventions stagnates, will technological advancement do the same?

In Chapter 3, I will present empirical evidence that suggests that an *Experiences → Inventive Ideas* paradigm has construct validity across federal agencies—a federal agency, the aggregation unit of its federal laboratories, being the data-specific focus of this book. I quantify *Experiences* in terms of the number of STEM (Science, Technology, Engineering, and Mathematics) colleagues with whom scientists and researchers interact in the federal laboratories. My empirical analyses in this chapter show that in some federal agencies the *Experiences → Inventive Ideas* relationship, so measured, is stronger (in a statistical sense) than in others. This chapter concludes with the interpretative question as to why some agencies are more efficient in the process of creating new inventive ideas, that is: Why are some agencies more efficient in an *Experiences → Inventive Ideas* process than others?

In Chapter 4, I will offer a conceptual as well as empirical answer to the question about why some agencies are more efficient in the process of creating new inventive ideas. The answer, as the reader might already expect, is that the scientists and researchers in some agencies have more technical capital, that is more R&D (research and development) resources, with which to work, than do the scientists and researchers in other agencies. This chapter concludes with affirmation of the relationship in equation (1.2) above: *Inventive Ideas = f (HC, TC)*. And I posit that this relationship may be closer to the knowledge production function than what has been reported in the literature, which was spawned by Zvi Griliches's 1979 seminal paper. The knowledge production function that is often estimated in the academic literature is described mathematically in the appendix at the end of this chapter.

In Chapter 5, I will add to the extant literature through empirical analyses of what I call an *enhanced knowledge production function*. Specifically, I offer evidence in support of the statistical significance of the relationship: *Patent Applications = G (Inventive Ideas)*. And I will posit that this relationship has policy relevance. If patent applications are a first step through which new scientific knowledge is formally developed in federal laboratories so that it can eventually be transferred to society through licensed patented inventions, and if such enhanced technology transfer is a national policy goal—which President Obama's Memorandum and President Trump's *Agenda* cited above clearly suggest that it is—then inventive ideas are a relevant national policy target variable.

In Chapter 6, I will present a case study of the *Patent Applications = G (Inventive Ideas)* relationship using invention disclosures information from one federal laboratory: the National Institute of Standards and Technology (NIST) within the U.S. Department of Commerce.

In Chapter 7, I will depart a bit from a focus on patent applications as a relevant technology transfer mechanism, and examine another technology transfer mechanism, namely cooperative research and development agreement (CRADA) activities. The relationship that I explore in this chapter is *CRADAs = G (Inventive Ideas)*. I couch the non-significant statistical findings in this chapter in the context of the economic concepts of market failure and government failure.

Finally, in Chapter 8, I will offer a brief summary of the findings presented in this book. I also expand on policy recommendations for enhancement of scientific ideas with particular reference to President Trump's *The President's Management Agenda*, and I suggest a future research agenda that emphasizes not only unexplored technology transfer activities in federal laboratories, but also other areas of research related to an *Experiences → Inventive Ideas* paradigm.

APPENDIX ON KNOWLEDGE PRODUCTION FUNCTIONS

The general form for an estimable knowledge production function is, following Hall and Ziedonis (2001) and Czarnitski, Kraft, and Thorwarth (2009):

$$PatApp = A\ RD^{\alpha}\ L^{\beta} \tag{A.1}$$

where *PatApp* is the count of new patent applications, A is a constant or disembodied shift factor, *RD* represents R&D investments, *L* represents the number of employees, and α and β measure the contribution of each input to the production of patent applications.

Equation (A.1) can be rewritten in two ways. Taking the natural logarithm in equation (A.1) yields:

$$log\ (PatApp) = log\ (A) + (\alpha{+}\beta{+}\gamma)\ log\ (L) + \alpha\ log\ (RD/L) \tag{A.2}$$

Alternatively, equation (A.1) itself can be rewritten as:

$$PatApp = exp(log\ (A) + (\alpha{+}\beta{+}\gamma)\ log\ (L) + \alpha\ log\ (RD/L)) \tag{A.3}$$

Equations (A.2) and (A.3) represent the traditional framework for the estimation of a public sector knowledge production function. More generally, the production function for patent applications may be unknown, so that estimating equations such as (A.2) and (A.3) cannot be derived. In this case, it may be of interest to estimate a semi- or non-parametric regression model for patent applications.

Equation (A.2) is often estimated by an Ordinary Least Squares (OLS) regression, using those observations for which the logarithms are well defined. Equation (A.3) is often estimated by a Poisson or negative binomial regression.

In addition to the research by Hall and Ziedonis (2001) and Czarnitski, Kraft, and Thorwarth (2009), see Link, Morris, and Van Hasselt (2019), Link and Van Hasselt (2019), Link (2019), and Link and Oliver (2020).

NOTES

1. According to U.S. Code, Title 15 (Chapter 63, § 3703): "Federal laboratory means any laboratory, any federally funded research and development center, or any center ... that is owned, leased, or otherwise used by a Federal agency and funded by the Federal Government, whether operated by the Government or by a contractor ... Federal agency means any executive agency ... as well as any agency of the legislative branch of the Federal Government." The phrase "national laboratories" refers to mission-driven research centers, and they are generally federally funded research and development centers (FFRDCs) or Government Owned, Contractor Operated (GOCO) laboratories. "Contractor operated labs ... operate facilities and equipment that are owned by the federal government, but the staff is employed by a private or nonprofit contractor that operates the lab under a contract with the federal government" (GAO, 2018, p. 10). The phrase "federal laboratories" refers to Government Owned, Government Operated (GOGO) laboratories. "Government operated labs are usually owned or leased by the federal government and are predominantly staffed by federal employees" (GAO, 2018, p. 10). There are different estimates of the number of federal laboratories in the United States. One lower bound estimate comes from the Federal Laboratory Consortium (FLC), which counts as its members more than 300 federal laboratories (FLC, 2017).
2. There may also be a related literature by philosophers who write about epistemology. I yield to these scholars to present that important body of thought.
3. I confess that data availability was in fact a factor in the knowledge production studies in which I was involved (e.g., Link, 2019; Link and Van Hasselt, 2019; Link, Morris, and Van Hasselt, 2019; and Link and Oliver, 2020).
4. This discussion about John Locke draws from Audretsch and Link (2019).
5. See https://ww.Brainyquote.com/quotes/albert_einstein_148788 (accessed July 3, 2020).
6. See https://en.wikiquote.org/wiki/Alfred_Nobel (accessed July 3, 2020).
7. An important point. I am using the symbol → throughout this book as a shorthand for the phrase *is related to*. I will use this symbol many times in later chapters to refer to how I suggest one interprets selected regression results. I am not using this → symbol to emphasize a causal relationship, although the relationships that I estimate, and which are described in Figure 2.2 in the following Chapter 2, do suggest causality in terms of the technology transfer process in federal laboratories.
8. I discuss, along with Dennis Leyden (Leyden and Link, 2015), this concept of experience in terms of networks, specifically weak ties and strong ties within an entrepreneur's or entrepreneurial firm's social network. See also Acemoglu, Akcigit, and Kerr (2016, p. 11483) who write about, although in the context of patents, the importance of networks in the following way: "Technological and scientific progress propels economic growth and long-term well-being. Prominent

theories depict this process as a cumulative one in which new innovations build on past achievements, using Newton's descriptive phrase of 'standing on the shoulders of giants.' … [T]he idea that when there is more past innovation for a particular technology class to build on, then that technology class innovates more."

9. Caveats aside, I now formally invoke the usual disclaimer that the proxy for experiences that I am suggesting is the best measure for a set of one's experiences that is available to me within the realm of technology transfer mechanisms, metrics, and related activities in federal laboratories. In a very specific sense, the availability of data is driving my arguments here, as I suspect it has with others who have studied the technology transfer process in federal laboratories, as well as driving the analyses that I present in the following chapters of this book.

10. The following section draws from Link and Scott (2018) and Link (2020).

11. In other words, the new millennium and the ICT revolution presented both challenges and opportunities regarding employment growth and the proximity of a science and technology park.

12. On a related note, and drawing from scholars in the field of geography, Ballard, Jara-Figueroa, Petralia, Steijn, Rigby, and Hidalgo (2020, p. 8) offer the following argument for why complex ideas concentrate in big cities. They write: "We argue that complex economic activities tend to be more concentrated in large urban areas because they require a deeper division of knowledge and labor. This also tells us that much of the (tacit) knowledge needed to perform these activities is embodied in social networks and that does not travel well through digital communication channels." I believe that this idea complements the agglomeration benefits noted above to the extent that the number of one's research colleagues proxies the complexity of ideas with which one is surrounded. It also underscores my emphasis on *Experiences*.

13. Zack Oliver and I (Link and Oliver, 2020) have offered a strong argument that data availability is the culprit that has limited studies of technology transfer in federal laboratories in both the United States and elsewhere. Relevant literature reviews are presented in Link and Oliver (2020) and, to a more limited extent, in Bozeman (2000). See also endnote 9 above.

14. See https://www.history.com/topics/world-war-ii/atomic-bomb-history#section_2 (accessed July 3, 2020).

15. See https://www.lanl.gov/ (accessed July 3, 2020).

16. According to the Bureau of Labor Statistics (BLS): "[P]roductivity growth has the potential to lead to improved living standards for those participating in an economy, in the form of higher income, greater leisure time, or a mixture of both. With gains in labor productivity, an economy is able to produce increasingly more goods and services for a given number of hours of work. These gains in efficiency make it possible for an economy to achieve growth in labor income, profits and capital gains of businesses, and public sector revenue. Moreover, as labor productivity grows, it may be possible for all of these factors to increase simultaneously, without gains in one coming at the cost of one of the others." See https://www.bls.gov/opub/btn/volume-6/below-trend-the-us-productivity-slowdown-since-the-great-recession.htm (accessed July, 2020).

17. In fact, it is my view that President Obama's Memorandum was the salvo to initiate others to pay closer research attention to technology transfer activity in federal laboratories. See, for example, the RTI International study, commissioned by the National Institute of Standard and Technology (NIST), conducted by Link,

Oliver, Jordan, and Hayter (2019). Also, the Board on Science and Technology Policy at the National Academies (the National Academy of Sciences, the National Academy of Engineering, and the Institute of Medicine) recently commissioned a study on Advancing Commercialization from the Federal Laboratories (see https://sites.nationalacademies.org/PGA/step/PGA_191994, accessed July 3, 2020).

18. I will elaborate on the policy importance of President Trump's *The President's Management Agenda* in Chapter 8.

2. New invention disclosures

LEGISLATIVE BACKGROUND

According to the U.S. Code of Federal Regulations (37 C.F.R. §501.3(d)), an invention is defined as "any art or process, machine, manufacture, design, or composition of matter, or any new and useful improvement thereof, or any variety of plant, which is or may be patentable under the patent laws of the United States."[1] An understanding of the term invention has legislative significance, as I explain below.

As succinctly written in a June 2018 United States Government Accounting Office (GAO) Report to the Chairman, Committee on the Judiciary, House of Representatives entitled "FEDERAL RESEARCH: Additional Actions Needed to Improve Licensing of Patented Laboratory Inventions":

> Prior to 1980, federal agencies generally retained title to any inventions developed through federally funded research—whether extramural, that is, conducted by universities and contractors, or intramural, conducted by federal agencies in their own facilities. By the late 1970s, there was increasing debate in Congress over ways to allow the private and public sectors better access to federally owned inventions by, among other things, creating a uniform policy for those seeking to license inventions developed in federal labs. In the 1980s, Congress began passing a series of key laws that have provided the foundation for federal technology transfer activities, including patenting and licensing inventions that are developed in federal labs and funded by federal dollars. One of the first technology transfer laws, the Stevenson-Wydler Act, established technology transfer as a federal policy and required federal labs to set up Offices of Research and Technology Applications (which, for our purposes, we refer to as technology transfer offices) and devote budget and personnel resources to promoting the transfer of federal technologies to the private sector.

Dennis Leyden and I (2015) have previously argued (and our view has not changed) that the Stevenson-Wydler Technology Innovation Act of 1980 (Public Law 96–480) was one of several important Congressional responses to the productivity slowdown that plagued the U.S. economy in the early 1970s and again in the late 1970s and early 1980s. Figure 2.1 shows the multifactor productivity (MFP) index, normalized to 2009 (2009 = 100), for the private U.S. business sector over the years 1948 through 2017.[2] The years of the productivity slowdown are highlighted by the darkened vertical bars. Note that the Stevenson-Wydler Act of 1980 was passed toward the end of the second productivity slowdown period highlighted in Figure 2.1.[3]

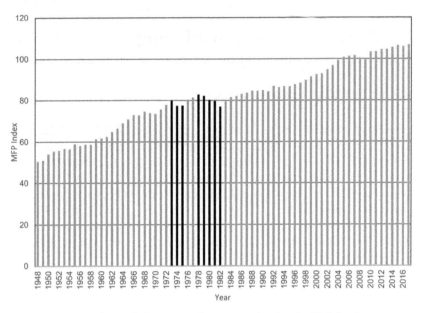

Figure 2.1   *The multifactor productivity index for the U.S. business
                   sector (1948–2017)*

Source: https://www.bls.gov/mfp/tables.htm (accessed August 3, 2020).

The Stevenson-Wydler Act of 1980 encouraged the transfer of federally developed technology:

> It is the continuing responsibility of the Federal Government to ensure the full use of the results of the Nation's Federal investment in research and development. To this end the Federal Government shall strive where appropriate to transfer federally owned or originated technology to State and local governments and to the private sector. Technology transfer, consistent with mission responsibilities, is a responsibility of each laboratory science and engineering professional.

To facilitate this technology transfer mission responsibility, the Act required:

> Each Federal laboratory shall establish an Office of Research and Technology Applications. Laboratories having existing organizational structures which perform the functions of this section may elect to combine the Office of Research and Technology Applications within the existing organization. The staffing and funding

levels for these offices shall be determined between each Federal laboratory and the Federal agency operating or directing the laboratory, except that (1) each laboratory having 200 or more full-time equivalent scientific, engineering, and related technical positions shall provide one or more full-time equivalent positions as staff for its Office of Research and Technology Applications, and (2) each Federal agency which operates or directs one or more Federal laboratories shall make available sufficient funding, either as a separate line item or from the agency's research and development budget, to support the technology transfer function at the agency and at its laboratories, including support of the Offices of Research and Technology Applications. Furthermore, individuals filling positions in an Office of Research and Technology Applications shall be included in the overall laboratory/agency management development program so as to ensure that highly competent technical managers are full participants in the technology transfer process.

As described in the 2018 GAO report, the genesis of the process of transferring a federal technology begins with the laboratory scientist or researcher completing an invention disclosure form and then submitting it to his or her technology transfer office (TTO). The GAO report illustrates the technology transfer process in terms of a diagram similar to that shown in Figure 2.2.[4] The eventual output from invention disclosures shown in the figure is the licensing of a patented invention or technology.[5,6] Of course, prerequisite to the licensing of an invention or technology is the patent itself. And a patent application obviously precedes a patent being issued much less a patented technology being licensed and thus put into use (an innovation is a technology put into use, i.e., commercialized).

The Stevenson-Wydler Act of 1980 was later amended by the Federal Technology Transfer Act of 1986 (Public Law 99-502). This amendment, among other things, established the Federal Laboratory Consortium (FLC):[7]

> There is hereby established the Federal Laboratory Consortium for Technology Transfer (hereinafter referred to as the "Consortium") which, in cooperation with Federal Laboratories and the private sector, shall—
> (A) develop and (with the consent of the Federal laboratory concerned) administer techniques, training courses, and materials concerning technology transfer to increase the awareness of Federal laboratory employees regarding the commercial potential of laboratory technology and innovations,
> (B) furnish advice and assistance requested by Federal agencies and laboratories for use in their technology transfer programs (including the planning of seminars for small business and other industry),
> (C) provide a clearinghouse for requests, received at the laboratory level, for technical assistance from States and units of local governments, businesses, industrial development organizations, not-for-profit organizations including universities, Federal agencies and laboratories, and other persons ...

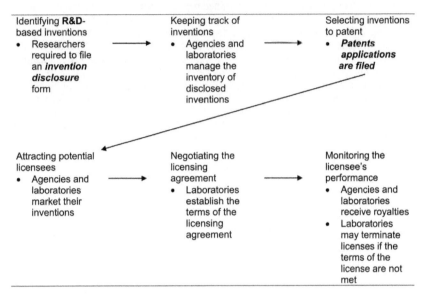

Figure 2.2   The invention disclosures to patent licensing process

Source: Based on GAO (2018, p. 11).

To emphasize the national importance of technology transfer from federal laboratories, the Federal Technology Transfer Act stated:

> Each laboratory director shall ensure that efforts to transfer technology are considered positively in laboratory job descriptions, employee promotion policies, and evaluation of the job performance of scientists and engineers in the laboratory.

And:[8]

> The head of the agency or his designee shall pay at least 15 percent of the royalties or other income the agency receives on account of any invention to the inventor (or co-inventors) if the inventor (or each such co-inventor) was an employee of the agency at the time the invention was made.

RESPONSE TO A MARKET FAILURE

One might reasonably ask why the federal government is involved in R&D activity that will lead to a technology that will possibly be licensed to others, where the categorical term "others" includes private sector firms as well as public and private sector organizations. And it is those in the category of "others" that pay federal taxes that are used to operate, at least in part, the federal laboratories from which the inventions originate that lead to a technology license.

In a sense, then, the federal government's R&D activity, which is paid for with public moneys, may be thought of as a response to a market failure. That is, the private sector has underinvested in those technologies for which the public sector views as socially desirable.[9]

John Scott and I (Link and Scott, 2011) have shown that this type of situation can result when the private sector's rate of return to an R&D project is less than the private sector's hurdle rate (i.e., the private sector's minimum acceptable rate of return on an R&D investment), and when the public sector's rate of return to the same R&D project is greater than the public sector's hurdle rate. Thus, the R&D, especially non-defense-oriented R&D, conducted in federal laboratories is explained by a market failure argument. I will return to this market failure argument in Chapter 7.

INVENTION DISCLOSURES OVER TIME

Each agency's TTO, and sometimes the laboratories within an agency have their own technology transfer infrastructure and office, has its own unique invention disclosure form.[10] From these forms, each agency for each fiscal year, on behalf of its laboratories, submits to the Technology Partnerships Office at the National Institute of Standards and Technology (NIST) a technology transfer report that includes information and metrics on various technology transfer mechanisms aggregated across that agency's laboratories. New invention disclosures are one of these technology transfer mechanisms reported in each agency's annual technology transfer report. The Technology Partnerships Office publishes each year the *Federal Laboratory Technology Transfer [Fiscal Year]: Summary Report to the President and the Congress.*[11] This annual report summarizes all of the agencies' annual reports.

Table 2.1 shows the number of new invention disclosures for each of the 11 reporting agencies for each fiscal year (FY) over the period FY 2003 through FY 2015.[12] The statistical analyses in this chapter, and in fact throughout this book, should be interpreted with caution because the number of fiscal years of data on invention disclosures, and for metrics for other technology transfer mechanisms as well, for each agency is limited as seen from Table 2.1.[13,14] Albeit that the data in the table are limited in terms of the number of fiscal years for which information is available, the analyses that follow are among the very few that are focused on—focused on with emphasis, I might add—invention disclosures in federal laboratories. Therefore, even descriptive analyses of these data might motivate future research on the topic of inventive ideas or even specific laboratory by laboratory research using a case study level methodology.[15,16]

Table 2.1 New invention disclosures by agency and by fiscal year, FY 2003–FY 2015

Agency	FY 2003	FY 2004	FY 2005	FY 2006	FY 2007	FY 2008	FY 2009	FY 2010	FY 2011	FY 2012	FY 2013	FY 2014	FY 2015
USDA	121	142	125	105	126	100	178	149	158	160	191	117	222
DOC	21	25	21	14	32	40	40	31	26	52	41	47	61
DOD	1332	1369	534	1056	838	1018	831	698	929	1078	1032	963	781
DOE	1469	1617	1776	1694	1575	1460	1439	1616	1820	1661	1796	1588	1645
HHS	472	461	452	442	447	437	353	337	351	352	320	351	321
DHS	–	–	–	–	10	10	32	7	38	40	20	36	15
DOI	9	6	4	5	7	7	4	5	5	10	9	6	7
DOT	0	0	4	3	2	3	3	1	2	2	13	3	0
VA	183	204	165	157	175	164	150	171	191	335	273	290	221
EPA	14	18	12	12	16	9	8	5	8	18	8	5	7
NASA	1485	1612	1682	1749	1514	1324	1412	1735	1748	1656	1627	1701	1550

Note: Agencies are listed in this and in the following tables in the order in which they are presented by the Technology Partnerships Office in its annual reports and in its summary tables.

Source: Technology Partnerships Office at NIST, https://www.nist.gov/tpo/reports-and-publications (accessed August 3, 2020).

Key:
USDA: U.S. Department of Agriculture
DOC: Department of Commerce
DOD: Department of Defense
DOE: Department of Energy
HHS: Health and Human Services
DHS: Department of Homeland Security
DOI: Department of Interior
DOT: Department of Transportation
VA: Department of Veterans Affairs
EPA: Environmental Protection Agency
NASA: National Aeronautics and Space Administration

A visual inspection of the number of invention disclosures in Table 2.1 suggests that inventiveness has been increasing over some of the fiscal years for which data are available, in some agencies but not in all years or in all agencies. For example, visually, there appears to be a general upward trend in invention disclosures at the U.S. Department of Agriculture (USDA) and at the Department of Commerce (DOC); there appears to be a downward trend at the Department of Defense (DOD), at Health and Human Services (HHS), and at the Environmental Protection Agency (EPA). The trend pattern at the other agencies is sporadic. These agency by agency trend patterns are shown more clearly in Figures 2.3 through 2.13.[17]

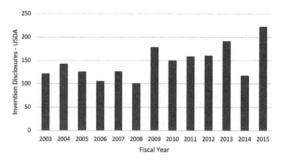

Figure 2.3   *Invention disclosures at the U.S. Department of Agriculture (USDA), FY 2003–FY 2015*

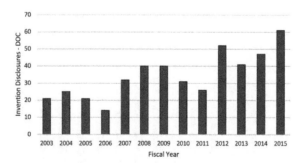

Figure 2.4   *Invention disclosures at the Department of Commerce (DOC), FY 2003–FY 2015*

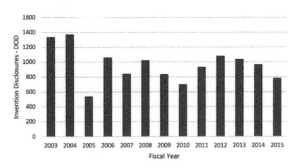

Figure 2.5   *Invention disclosures at the Department of Defense (DOD),*
                  FY 2003–FY 2015

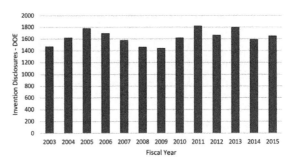

Figure 2.6   *Invention disclosures at the Department of Energy (DOE),*
                  FY 2003–FY 2015

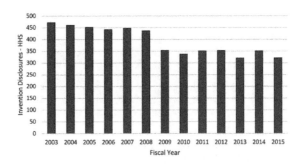

Figure 2.7   *Invention disclosures at Health and Human Services (HHS),*
                  FY 2003–FY 2015

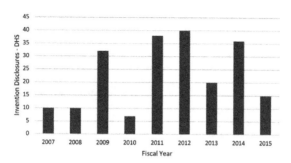

Figure 2.8   *Invention disclosures at the Department of Homeland Security (DHS), FY 2007–FY 2015*

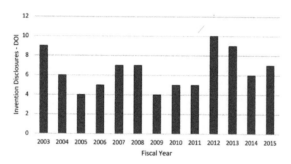

Figure 2.9   *Invention disclosures at the Department of Interior (DOI), FY 2003–FY 2015*

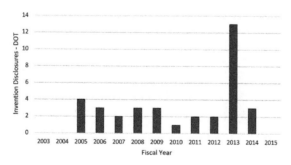

Figure 2.10   *Invention disclosures at the Department of Transportation (DOT), FY 2003–FY 2015*

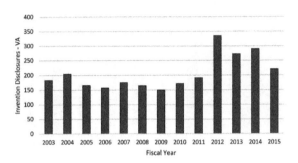

Figure 2.11   *Invention disclosures at the Department of Veterans Affairs (VA), FY 2003–FY 2015*

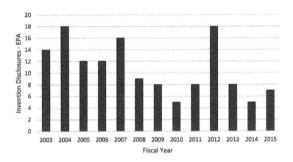

Figure 2.12   *Invention disclosures at the Environmental Protection Agency (EPA), FY 2003–FY 2015*

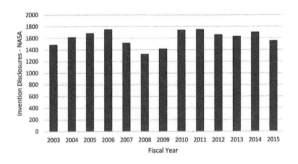

Figure 2.13   *Invention disclosures at the National Aeronautics and Space Administration (NASA), FY 2003–FY 2015*

An inspection of Figures 2.3 through 2.13 supports my generalizations just above, and it reveals at least two interesting patterns across agencies. First, the Great Recession (documented as occurring from December 2007 through June 2009) appears to have had an impact on invention disclosures in a number of agencies. For example, at the Department of Energy (Figure 2.6), invention disclosures fell from FY 2005 through FY 2009, perhaps in anticipation of a pending recession, but they rebounded in FY 2010 and FY 2011. More pronounced than at the Department of Energy was the decline in invention disclosures at Health and Human Services (Figure 2.7) from FY 2008 to FY 2009, but there was no rebound to a pre-Great Recession level of invention disclosures. At the Department of Interior (Figure 2.9), invention disclosures declined significantly (in a visual sense) from FY 2008 to FY 2009, but they did not rebound until FY 2012. Invention disclosures declined only slightly from FY 2007 through FY 2009 at the Department of Veterans Affairs (Figure 2.11), but they quickly rebounded. The decline in invention disclosures at the Environmental Protection Agency (Figure 2.12) was very pronounced during the Great Recession, but they rebounded in FY 2011 and in FY 2012, and then declined again. Finally, invention disclosures began to decline after FY 2006 at the National Aeronautics and Space Administration (Figure 2.13), and they did not recover until 2010.

Second, there has not been a consistent trend pattern across agencies in invention disclosures in the post-Great Recession years. For example, at the Department of Commerce (Figure 2.4), invention disclosures have increased since FY 2013; in comparison, at the Department of Defense (Figure 2.5), invention disclosures have decreased since FY 2012; and at other agencies the recent trend pattern is mixed.

More formally, I estimated the trend pattern in invention disclosures over time using the following regression model:[18]

$$Invention\ Disclosures = \alpha + \beta 1\ Year + Agency\ Controls + \varepsilon \qquad (2.1)$$

where the variable *Year* is a fiscal year counter from FY 2003 through FY 2015, $\beta 1$ is the estimated slope of the *Invention Disclosures* trend line, *Agency Controls* account for agency fixed effects,[19] and ε is an error term assumed to obey all classical assumptions.

Descriptive statistics on *Invention Disclosures*, by agency, are in Table 2.2, and the regression results from the estimation of equation (2.1) are in Table 2.3.

Table 2.2   Descriptive statistics for the dependent variable Invention Disclosures in equation (2.1)

Agency (observations)	Mean	Standard Deviation	Minimum	Maximum
USDA (n = 13)	145.69	35.70	100	222
DOC (n = 13)	34.69	13.64	14	61
DOD (n = 13)	958.38	233.09	534	1369
DOE (n = 13)	1627.38	124.71	1439	1820
HHS (n = 13)	392	59.19	320	472
DHS (n = 9)	23.11	13.37	7	40
DOI (n = 13)	6.46	1.94	4	10
DOT (n = 13)	2.77	3.35	0	13
VA (n = 13)	206.08	57.98	150	335
EPA (n = 13)	10.77	4.59	5	18
NASA (n = 13)	1599.62	134.75	1324	1749

Source: Table 2.1.
Key:
USDA: U.S. Department of Agriculture
DOC: Department of Commerce
DOD: Department of Defense
DOE: Department of Energy
HHS: Health and Human Services
DHS: Department of Homeland Security
DOI: Department of Interior
DOT: Department of Transportation
VA: Department of Veterans Affairs
EPA: Environmental Protection Agency
NASA: National Aeronautics and Space Administration

As shown in Table 2.3, the estimated slope coefficient from equation (2.1), $\beta1$, is positive, but it is not statistically different from zero.[20] In other words, over the period of FY 2003 through FY 2015, inventions disclosures in the agencies studied (i.e., in the agencies for which invention disclosure data are available) have been, on average, flat in a statistical sense. That regression result is perhaps not unexpected given the visual trend pattern in the total number of invention disclosures across all agencies by fiscal years suggested by Figure 2.14.[21]

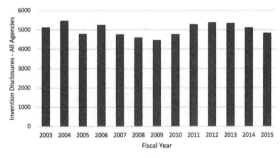

Figure 2.14   Invention disclosures at all agencies, FY 2003–FY 2015

Table 2.3   *Regression results from equation (2.1), dependent variable is Invention Disclosures (standard errors in parentheses)*

Independent Variable	Regression Coefficient
Year	0.5081
	(2.2794)
USDA	124.1228***
	(41.7435)
DOC	16.5493
	(41.7151)
DOD	931.4546***
	(41.7152)
DOE	1607.0***
	(41.7154)
HHS	369.0528***
	(41.7129)
DOI	-15.4567
	(41.9857)
DOT	-19.2937
	(41.7122)
VA	182.8714***
	(41.7152)
EPA	-9.6966
	(41.7153)
NASA	1575.0***
	(41.7259)
Intercept	-998.6787
	(4584.0)
n	139
R^2	0.9794

Notes:
*** significant at .01 level.
The Department of Homeland Security (DHS) is subsumed in the intercept term.
Autocorrelation corrections were done using the Yule-Walker method. My implicit assumption is that the autoregressive pattern in the error terms is constant across agencies.
Key:
USDA: U.S. Department of Agriculture
DOC: Department of Commerce
DOD: Department of Defense
DOE: Department of Energy
HHS: Health and Human Services
DHS: Department of Homeland Security
DOI: Department of Interior
DOT: Department of Transportation
VA: Department of Veterans Affairs
EPA: Environmental Protection Agency
NASA: National Aeronautics and Space Administration

CONCLUDING OBSERVATION

There is a clever (and educationally useful, at least from my own classroom teaching experiences) TED Talk by Steven Johnson entitled "Where Good Ideas Come From"—the same title as his *New York Times* bestselling book from which I quoted in Chapter 1. In his talk, he describes the English coffee houses in the 1650s as places where individuals gather to talk and exchange thoughts and where "ideas come to have sex."[22] His message is that "an idea is a network," and my interpretation of that message in the context of this chapter, and for that matter in this book, is that ideas beget ideas.[23] If scientific ideas do beget scientific ideas, and if new ideas, that is new invention disclosures, lead to new patent applications in the sense of Figure 2.2, then I conclude this chapter with the question: What does it say about the effective use of federal laboratory R&D expenditures, which is part of the technical capital (*TC*) referred to in the equations in Chapter 1 and which is conducted in part to overcome a market failure, over time given that new inventive ideas have not been increasing over time?

Anticipating a policy point that I will again raise in the concluding Chapter 8, especially with reflection on Figure 2.2, is if new inventive ideas do not increase over time then patentable technologies might cease to increase over time, and knowledge transferred from federal laboratories to society through that mechanism might also possibly cease to increase over time.

NOTES

1. See https://ecfr.io/Title-37/se37.1.501_13 (accessed August 3, 2020).
2. The Bureau of Labor Statistics (BLS) prefers the term multifactor productivity (MFP), but economists frequently refer to this same concept as total factor productivity (TFP). According to the BLS: "Multifactor productivity (MFP), also known as total factor productivity (TFP), is a measure of economic performance that compares the amount of goods and services produced (output) to the amount of combined inputs used to produce those goods and services. Inputs can include labor, capital, energy, materials, and purchased services." See https://www.bls.gov/mfp/home.htm (accessed August 3, 2020).
3. Bozeman and Link (2015) make the case heuristically and empirically that the portfolio of productivity enhancing public policies in the early 1980s led to the resurgence in productivity growth in the late 1980s.
4. The points of emphasis in Figure 2.2 that are in bold type are my points of emphasis and not those of the GAO report authors.
5. A figure similar to that presented as Figure 2.2 is also in FLC (2013).
6. In Chapter 7, I will discuss CRADAs as another technology transfer mechanism.
7. A brief history of the Federal Laboratory Consortium (FLC) is in Link and Oliver (2020).
8. Link, Siegel, and Van Fleet (2011) showed empirically that patenting activity at the National Institute of Standards and Technology (NIST) and at Sandia

National Laboratories (Albuquerque, NM) did not increase after the passage of the Stevenson-Wydler Act of 1980, but it did increase after the passage of the Federal Technology Transfer Act of 1986. The authors suggested that the upturn in patenting activity was due, in part, to the financial incentives (i.e., royalty sharing with inventors) provided in the Federal Technology Transfer Act of 1986.

9. It is beyond the focus of this book to belabor a discussion about open source technology, although one could cast the conclusions from this book about the national economic growth related need for scientific ideas (i.e., invention disclosures) to increase over time rather than be flat over time. Bob Danziger, John Scott, and I have elsewhere (Link, Danziger, and Scott, 2018) made a case for a federally funded university-based pharmaceutical researcher, and their universities, embracing an open source position.

10. The National Institute of Standards and Technology (NIST) recently revised its invention disclosure form. See https://www.federalregister.gov/documents/2019/08/07/2019-16882/proposed-information-collection-nist-invention-disclosure-and-inventor-information-collection (accessed August 3, 2020).

11. Agency technology transfer reports and the Technology Partnerships Office reports are available at: https://www.nist.gov/tpo/reports-and-publications/annual-reports (accessed August 3, 2020).

12. These data come from the Technology Partnerships Office's annual reports.

13. I am dropping the adjective "new" when I write the term "invention disclosures," but I will include the adjective "new" from time to time for purposes of emphasis.

14. I have chosen to illustrate agency by agency relevant metrics in tables throughout this book, but the related statistical analyses only account for agency differences as reflected in fixed effects.

15. I thank my friend and long time virtual mentor, Professor Edwin Mansfield of the University of Pennsylvinia, for emphasizing to me on many occasions the importance of descriptive analyses even in an era of econometric sophistication. See Link and Scherer (2005).

16. One might reasonably think of a federal laboratory scientist or researcher as a public sector entrepreneur. He or she perceives an opportunity and acts on that perception through his or her participation in the disclosure process (see Hébert and Link, 2009 for a discussion of an entrepreneur as one who perceives an opportunity and then acts on that perception). A public sector entrepreneur within a federal laboratory does not imply that the federal laboratory is an example of public sector entrepreneurship as I have used and discussed the term in previous writings (e.g., Leyden and Link, 2015; Hayter, Link, and Scott, 2018; and Link and Oliver, 2020). Dennis Leyden and I (Leyden and Link, 2015, p. 46) defined the concept of public sector entrepreneurship in the following way: "Public sector entrepreneurship … refers to innovative public policy initiatives that generate greater economic prosperity by transforming a status quo economic environment into one that is more conducive to economic units engaging in creative activities in the face of uncertainty."

17. Data are available for the Department of Homeland Security (DHS) only for the fiscal years FY 2007 through FY 2015. The Department was formed in 2002.

18. Recall equation (1.2) from Chapter 1: *Inventive Ideas* = f (*HC*, *TC*). Measures of human capital (*HC*) and technical capital (*TC*) are not being held constant in the figures shown in this chapter or in the model in equation (2.1).

19. Fixed agency effects are used rather than agency clustered standard errors. Again, please note the limited number of years of data for the Department of Homeland Security (DHS).
20. The regression results from alternative specifications of equation (2.1) also show a statistically insignificant slope coefficient. In one alternative specification, the dependent variable was the natural logarithm of *Inventions Disclosures*. In other alternative specifications (linear and linear in logs) an additional independent variable was included. *Recession* = 1 for the years of the Great Recession (2008 and 2009) and 0 otherwise. Still, the estimated coefficient on *Year* was statistically insignificant.
21. The Great Recession dip in the trend pattern for invention disclosures is also evident in Figure 2.14.
22. See https://www.ted.com/talks/steven_johnson_where_good_ideas_come_from (accessed August 3, 2020).
23. I, along with my frequent co-author, David Audretsch, and my colleague Martijn van Hasselt (Audretsch, Link, and Van Hasselt, 2019) illustrated empirically that knowledge does in fact beget knowledge. We conclude that when a technology-based firm involves a university in its funded research projects, more scientific papers (i.e., scientific output) result from the firm's researchers.

3. Experiences and inventive ideas

STEM EMPLOYEES

In Chapter 1, I suggested that the study of inventive ideas might be framed in terms of an *Experiences → Inventive Ideas* paradigm, and in the previous chapter I offered invention disclosures as a possible metric for *Inventive Ideas*. In this chapter, I offer some supportive observational evidence to support the relationship in federal agencies between invention disclosures and experiences. The first step toward this observational evidence is to establish a metric for *Experiences*.

The acronym STEM refers to Science, Technology, Engineering, and Mathematics.[1] Many students of public policy, in general, and educational policy, in particular, point to a 1983 report prepared by President Ronald Reagan's National Commission on Excellence in Education entitled *A Nation at Risk: The Imperative for Educational Reform* as one of the initial documents associated with, as it has been called, the phrase *STEM movement*. More recently, the 2007 report by the National Academies (the National Academy of Sciences, the National Academy of Engineering, and the Institute of Medicine), entitled *Rising Above the Gathering Storm: Energizing and Employing America for a Brighter Economic Future*, addresses the so-called STEM crisis head on. One of the recommendations offered in the report *Rising Above the Gathering Storm* (p. 112) is: "Increase America's talent pool by vastly improving K–12 science and mathematics education." The supporting argument given in the report for this recommendation is:

> The US system of public education must lay the foundation for developing a workforce that is literate in mathematics and science, among other subjects. It is the creative intellectual energy of our workforce that will drive successful innovation and create jobs for all citizens.

Because the invention and innovation focus of this book began with a discussion of the genesis of inventive ideas, *Inventive Ideas*, and the data being discussed and analysed in the following chapters relate to federal laboratories aggregated to the agency level, it seems to me that a case can be made that a relevant measure to consider for experiences, *Experiences*, is the number of scientists and researchers that are classified as STEM employees with whom the scientists and researchers in an agency work.[2] This is not to say that other employees working in a laboratory within an agency are not valuable when it comes to initiating, fostering, or improving creativity or inventive ideas; rather, I am simply assuming that a larger portion of STEM employees would play that role than would non-STEM employees.[3]

To temper my assumption, although not to change it, about using the number of STEM employees to measure the experience base of laboratories within a federal agency at a specific point in time (i.e., in a fiscal year), I am reminded of the day when the new director of the equally new technology transfer office (TTO) at my home institution made a presentation to an assemblage of faculty. His assignment was, from the perspective of the university's hierarchy, to set the groundwork for future efforts by the administration to encourage faculty to undertake more applied research that could then lead to results that could eventually be patented by my university and then licensed to regional firms.[4] The potential for additional financial resources for the university was a motivating factor or force for this new strategic direction, as was a strategic goal of the university to be more involved in regional economic development.

The year was 2003, although the Bayh-Dole Act was legislated in 1980.[5] Our new director, after being introduced by the Provost, reflected on his prior experience as the director of a TTO at another university. In an effort to illustrate to the faculty that ideas, that is, disclosable inventions, can come from all parts of the university, and thus to suggest that any one in attendance could develop a disclosable invention, he told the assembled faculty that at his prior institution more invention disclosure forms were filled out and then submitted to the TTO by individuals who were in the unit on campus that started with the letter *P*. Then, he asked the faculty to guess which unit this might have been. The faculty were uncharacteristically silent! He then said: "What if I tell you the unit on campus filling out and submitting the most invention disclosure forms started with the letters *Ph*?" One person (who forever will remain unnamed!) shouted out "Psychology," then another shouted out, "Physics." The director said "no" to both; he said it was "Physical plant." Again, his point was that inventive ideas come from myriad and often unexpected sources and places. Still, I am sticking with STEM employees as the proxy for *Experiences* in this chapter and in the remaining chapters.

TREND PATTERNS IN EXPERIENCES

Consider the data in Table 3.1 on the number of STEM employees working in the United States, by agency and by fiscal year.[6] I have illustrated the trend pattern in these data in Figures 3.1 through 3.11. Overall, the trend pattern has been sporadic, but in the aggregate, it has been increasing. For example, at the Department of Commerce (Figure 3.2), the number of STEM employees increased each year through FY 2010 (i.e., throughout the Great Recession), and then decreased. The trend pattern in the number of STEM employees at the Department of Defense (Figure 3.3) has steadily increased over time. The trend pattern in the number of STEM employees has also steadily increased at Health and Human Services (Figure 3.5), at the Department of Homeland Security (Figure 3.6), at the Department of Transportation (Figure 3.8) until 2010, and at the Department of Veterans Affairs (Figure 3.9). In contrast, the trend pattern in the number of STEM employees at the U.S. Department of Agriculture (Figure 3.1) and at the Department of Interior (Figure 3.7) has, over all fiscal years, been decreasing, as it has in recent years at both the Environmental Protection Agency (Figure 3.10) and at the National Aeronautics and Space Administration (Figure 3.11). Figure 3.12 shows the trend in the number of all STEM employees aggregated across all of the federal agencies shown in the figures. Again, the trend pattern is generally increasing with a slight decrease after FY 2011.

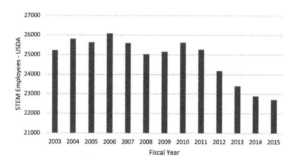

Figure 3.1   *STEM employees at the U.S. Department of Agriculture (USDA), FY 2003–FY 2015*

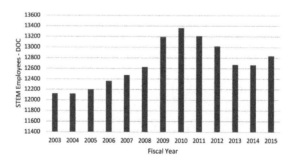

Figure 3.2   *STEM employees at the Department of Commerce (DOC), FY 2003–FY 2015*

Table 3.1   *STEM employees by agency and by fiscal year, FY 2003–FY 2015*

Agency	FY 2003	FY 2004	FY 2005	FY 2006	FY 2007	FY 2008	FY 2009	FY 2010	FY 2011	FY 2012	FY 2013	FY 2014	FY 2015
USDA	25 227	25 809	25 632	26 090	25 607	25 032	25 153	25 620	25 270	24 185	23 395	22 890	22 710
DOC	12 120	12 119	12 199	12 363	12 476	12 628	13 193	13 361	13 211	13 019	12 672	12 665	12 836
DOD	8 993	8 627	8 768	8 662	8 962	9 042	9 640	10 701	11 171	11 571	11 759	12 009	11 935
DOE	4 880	4 747	4 663	4 562	4 502	4 634	4 763	4 928	4 877	4 731	4 629	4 476	4 501
HHS	12 137	11 967	11 771	11 558	11 571	11 909	12 620	13 246	13 546	13 676	13 861	13 988	14 311
DHS	–	–	–	–	5 164	5 472	6 019	6 582	7 264	7 716	7 802	7 712	7 912
DOI	18 004	17 911	17 736	17 217	16 958	16 932	17 218	17 613	17 627	17 389	16 786	16 198	16 120
DOT	5 537	5 497	5 418	6 881	6 874	6 924	7 368	7 421	7 410	7 345	7 188	7 088	7 116
VA	6 508	6 905	7 110	7 146	7 254	7 654	8 072	8 487	8 920	9 052	9 210	9 197	9 370
EPA	7 517	7 630	7 612	7 664	7 679	7 809	7 929	8 092	8 081	7 848	7 472	7 020	6 908
NASA	11 017	11 355	11 173	11 109	11 244	11 485	11 555	11 751	11 821	11 594	11 564	11 430	11 214

Source: Office of Personnel Management, https://www.fedscope.opm.gov/employment.asp (accessed August 3, 2020).
Key:
USDA: U.S. Department of Agriculture
DOC: Department of Commerce
DOD: Department of Defense
DOE: Department of Energy
HHS: Health and Human Services
DHS: Department of Homeland Security
DOI: Department of Interior
DOT: Department of Transportation
VA: Department of Veterans Affairs
EPA: Environmental Protection Agency
NASA: National Aeronautics and Space Administration

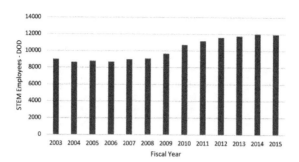

Figure 3.3   *STEM employees at the Department of Defense (DOD), FY 2003–FY 2015*

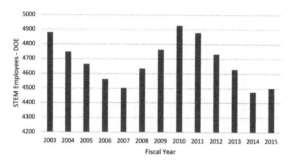

Figure 3.4   *STEM employees at the Department of Energy (DOE), FY 2003–FY 2015*

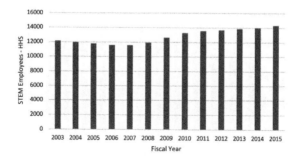

Figure 3.5   *STEM employees at Health and Human Services (HHS), FY 2003–FY 2015*

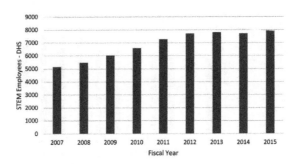

Figure 3.6 STEM employees at the Department of Homeland Security (DHS), FY 2007–FY 2015

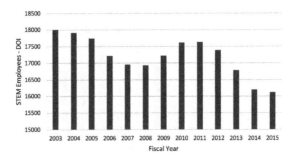

Figure 3.7 STEM employees at the Department of Interior (DOI), FY 2003–FY 2015

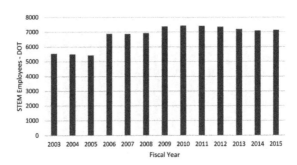

Figure 3.8 STEM employees at the Department of Transportation (DOT), FY 2003–FY 2015

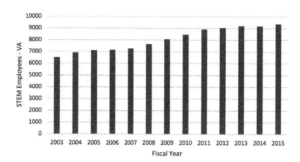

Figure 3.9   *STEM employees at the Department of Veterans Affairs (VA), FY 2003–FY 2015*

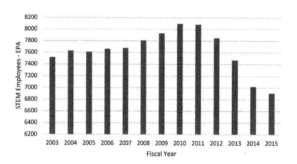

Figure 3.10   *STEM employees at the Environmental Protection Agency (EPA), FY 2003–FY 2015*

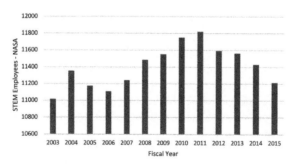

Figure 3.11   *STEM employees at the National Aeronautics and Space Administration (NASA), FY 2003–FY 2015*

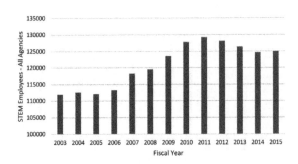

Figure 3.12   STEM employees at all agencies, FY 2003–FY 2015

Across all agencies, the source of ideas, that is, the STEM employees' experiences base which scientists and researchers draw on for their inventive ideas, has generally been increasing over time. This observation anticipates the question: If the source of inventive ideas (i.e., STEM employees) has generally been increasing over time, then why has the number of invention disclosures (i.e., inventive ideas), as shown in Chapter 2, been relatively flat over time? At first blush, one might answer this question by saying that perhaps the number of STEM employees is a poor measure of experiences, or by saying that other contributing factors have yet to be considered.

To be more formal about the trend pattern over time in STEM employees, as I did in Chapter 2 for invention disclosures, consider the following regression model:

$$STEM\ Employees = \alpha + \beta2\ Year + Agency\ Controls + \varepsilon \qquad (3.1)$$

where the independent variables and error term in equation (3.1) are as described in Chapter 2 with respect to equation (2.1).

Descriptive statistics on STEM Employees by agency are presented in Table 3.2, and the regression results from equation (3.1) are in Table 3.3.

The estimated slope coefficient, $\beta2$, from the estimation of equation (3.1) is positive and statistically different from zero as one might have inferred from Figure 3.12. On average, the increase in the number of STEM employees has been about 45 per year. The statistical finding about the slope coefficient being positive and statistically different from zero underscores the question that I raised above. To rephrase it and to ask yet another question: If the source of ideas, that is, the number of STEM employees, has been increasing over time but the number of inventive ideas, that is, the number of invention disclosures, has been remaining constant, what is going on? Is the process of *Experiences → Inventive Ideas* relevant across federal laboratories/agencies?

To investigate one possible answer to the questions just above about the relevance of the *Experiences → Inventive Ideas* paradigm for federal laboratories (i.e., If the source of inventive ideas has generally been increasing over time, then why has the number of invention disclosures been relatively flat over time?), consider the ratio of *Invention Disclosures to 100 STEM Employees* by agency and by fiscal year as shown in Table 3.4 and in Figures 3.13–3.23.

Table 3.2   *Descriptive statistics for the dependent variable STEM Employees in equation (3.1)*

Agency (observations)	Mean	Standard Deviation	Minimum	Maximum
USDA (n = 13)	24 816.92	1 141.80	22 710	26 090
DOC (n = 13)	12 681.69	423.57	12 119	13 361
DOD (n = 13)	10 141.54	1 392.74	8 627	12 009
DOE (n = 13)	4 684.08	152.30	4 476	4 928
HHS (n = 13)	12 781.62	1 016.95	11 558	14 311
DHS (n = 9)	6 849.22	1 072.52	5 164	7 912
DOI (n = 13)	17 208.38	598.59	16 120	18 004
DOT (n = 13)	6 774.38	760.07	5 418	7 421
VA (n = 13)	8 068.08	1 021.92	6 508	9 370
EPA (n = 13)	7 635.46	355.95	6 908	8 092
NASA (n = 13)	11 408.62	248.33	11 017	11 821

Source: Table 3.1.
Key:
USDA: U.S. Department of Agriculture
DOC: Department of Commerce
DOD: Department of Defense
DOE: Department of Energy
HHS: Health and Human Services
DHS: Department of Homeland Security
DOI: Department of Interior
DOT: Department of Transportation
VA: Department of Veterans Affairs
EPA: Environmental Protection Agency
NASA: National Aeronautics and Space Administration

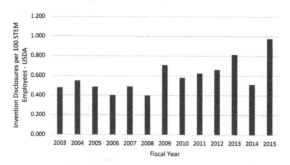

Figure 3.13   *Invention disclosures per 100 STEM employees at the U.S. Department of Agriculture (USDA), FY 2003– FY 2015*

Table 3.3   *Regression results from equation (3.1), dependent variable is STEM Employees (standard errors in parentheses)*

Independent Variable	Regression Coefficient
Year	44.9071***
	(9.9136)
USDA	17 527***
	(436.2013)
DOC	5 351***
	(323.4878)
DOD	2 703***
	(390.5402)
DOE	-3 382***
	(414.1146)
HHS	6 110***
	(428.2028)
DOI	10 130***
	(422.7236)
DOT	-264.6693
	(425.9440)
VA	1 351***
	(465.7670)
EPA	416.7168
	(427.2794)
NASA	3 480***
	(429.9550)
Intercept	-8 2993***
	(20010)
n	139
R^2	0.9964

Notes:
*** significant at .01 level.
The Department of Homeland Security (DHS) is subsumed in the intercept term.
Autocorrelation corrections were done using the Yule-Walker method. My implicit assumption is that the autoregressive pattern in the error terms is constant across agencies.
Key:
USDA: U.S. Department of Agriculture
DOC: Department of Commerce
DOD: Department of Defense
DOE: Department of Energy
HHS: Health and Human Services
DHS: Department of Homeland Security
DOI: Department of Interior
DOT: Department of Transportation
VA: Department of Veterans Affairs
EPA: Environmental Protection Agency
NASA: National Aeronautics and Space Administration

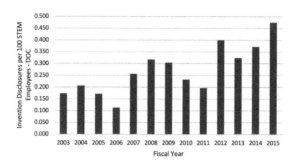

*Figure 3.14   Invention disclosures per 100 STEM employees at the
Department of Commerce (DOC), FY 2003–FY 2015*

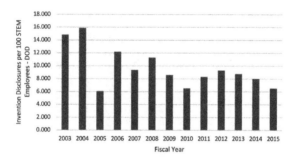

*Figure 3.15   Invention disclosures per 100 STEM employees at the
Department of Defense (DOD), FY 2003–FY 2015*

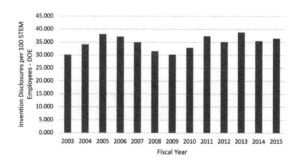

*Figure 3.16   Invention disclosures per 100 STEM employees at the
Department of Energy (DOE), FY 2003–FY 2015*

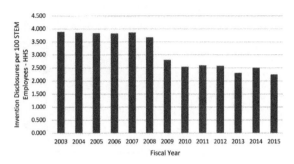

Figure 3.17   *Invention disclosures per 100 STEM employees at Health and Human Services HHS), FY 2003–FY 2015*

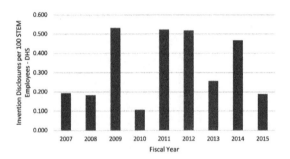

Figure 3.18   *Invention disclosures per 100 STEM employees at the Department of Homeland Security (DHS), FY 2007–FY 2015*

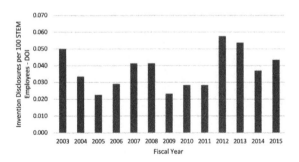

Figure 3.19   *Invention disclosures per 100 STEM employees at the Department of Interior (DOI), FY 2003–FY 2015*

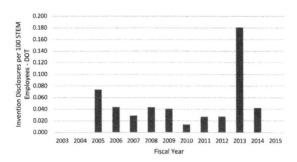

Figure 3.20 *Invention disclosures per 100 STEM employees at the Department of Transportation (DOT), FY 2003–FY 2015*

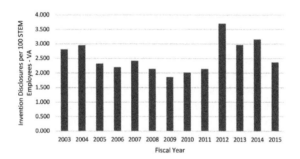

Figure 3.21 *Invention disclosures per 100 STEM employees at the Department of Veterans Affairs (VA), FY 2003–FY 2015*

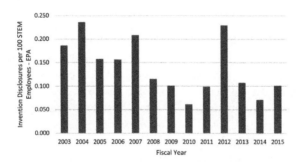

Figure 3.22 *Invention disclosures per 100 STEM employees at the Environmental Protection Agency (EPA), FY 2003–FY 2015*

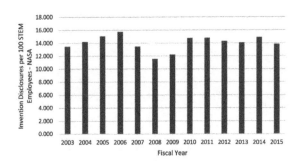

Figure 3.23   *Invention disclosures per 100 STEM employees at the National Aeronautics and Space Administration (NASA), FY 2003–FY 2015*

A visual comparison of agency trend patterns in the ratio of *Invention Disclosures to 100 STEM Employees* across agencies raises yet another question: Why is the ratio of *Invention Disclosures to 100 STEM Employees* greater and/or more volatile over time in some agencies compared to other agencies? Stated differently: Why are the laboratories in some agencies more effective in the *Experiences →️ Inventive Ideas* process than in other agencies? My asking this additional question does not dismiss the validity of the previously asked question: Is the process of *Experiences →️ Inventive Ideas* relevant across federal laboratories/agencies?

A visual inspection of Figures 3.12 through 3.23 emphasizes the pervasiveness of information that motivates the question about why the laboratories in some agencies are more effective in the *Experiences →️ Inventive Ideas* process (i.e., the STEM employees to invention disclosures relationship) than in other agencies. Over all fiscal years, the trend pattern in the ratio of *Invention Disclosures to 100 STEM Employees* is increasing only at the U.S. Department of Agriculture (Figure 3.13) and at the Department of Commerce (Figure 3.14). Across all of the fiscal years, the trend pattern is decreasing at the Department of Defense (Figure 3.15) and at Health and Human Services (Figure 3.16). The trend pattern in the other agencies is sporadic.

In Chapter 4, I offer a *possible* (my emphasis) answer to the questions posed above. For it was John Steinbeck who wrote in *Travels with Charley: In Search of America*: "A question is a trap, and an answer is your foot in it."[7] For now, I consider the trend pattern in the ratio of *Invention Disclosures to 100 STEM Employees* more formally through the following regression model:

$$Invention\ Disclosures\ per\ 100\ STEM\ Employees =$$
$$\alpha + \beta3\ Year + Agency\ Controls + \varepsilon \qquad (3.2)$$

Descriptive statistics on *Invention Disclosures per 100 STEM Employees* by agency are presented in Table 3.5, and the regression results from equation (3.2) are in Table 3.6.

Table 3.4   *Invention disclosures per 100 STEM employees by agency and by fiscal year, FY 2003–FY 2015*

Agency	FY 2003	FY 2004	FY 2005	FY 2006	FY 2007	FY 2008	FY 2009	FY 2010	FY 2011	FY 2012	FY 2013	FY 2014	FY 2015
USDA	0.480	0.550	0.488	0.402	0.492	0.399	0.708	0.582	0.625	0.662	0.816	0.511	0.978
DOC	0.173	0.206	0.172	0.113	0.256	0.317	0.303	0.232	0.197	0.399	0.324	0.371	0.475
DOD	14.812	15.869	6.090	12.191	9.351	11.259	8.620	6.523	8.316	9.316	8.776	8.019	6.544
DOE	30.102	34.064	38.087	37.133	34.984	31.506	30.212	32.792	37.318	35.109	38.799	35.478	36.547
HHS	3.889	3.852	3.840	3.824	3.863	3.669	2.797	2.544	2.591	2.574	2.309	2.509	2.243
DHS	–	–	–	–	0.194	0.183	0.532	0.106	0.523	0.518	0.256	0.467	0.190
DOI	0.050	0.033	0.023	0.029	0.041	0.041	0.023	0.028	0.028	0.058	0.054	0.037	0.043
DOT	0	0	0.074	0.044	0.029	0.043	0.041	0.013	0.027	0.027	0.181	0.042	0
VA	2.812	2.954	2.321	2.197	2.412	2.143	1.858	2.015	2.141	3.701	2.964	3.153	2.359
EPA	0.186	0.236	0.158	0.157	0.208	0.115	0.101	0.062	0.099	0.229	0.107	0.071	0.101
NASA	13.479	14.196	15.054	15.744	13.465	11.528	12.220	14.765	14.787	14.283	14.070	14.882	13.822

Source: Tables 2.1 and 3.1.

Key:
USDA: U.S. Department of Agriculture
DOC: Department of Commerce
DOD: Department of Defense
DOE: Department of Energy
HHS: Health and Human Services
DHS: Department of Homeland Security
DOI: Department of Interior
DOT: Department of Transportation
VA: Department of Veterans Affairs
EPA: Environmental Protection Agency
NASA: National Aeronautics and Space Administration

Table 3.5　　　*Descriptive statistics for Invention Disclosures per 100 STEM Employees in equation (3.2)*

Agency (observations)	Mean	Standard Deviation	Minimum	Maximum
USDA (n = 13)	0.5917	0.1666	0.3995	0.9775
DOC (n = 13)	0.2723	0.1040	0.1132	0.4752
DOD (n = 13)	9.6681	3.0676	6.0903	15.8688
DOE (n = 13)	34.7794	2.8976	30.1025	38.7989
HHS (n = 13)	3.1158	0.6958	2.2430	3.8889
DHS (n = 9)	0.3299	0.1759	0.1064	0.5316
DOI (n = 13)	0.0376	0.0114	0.0226	0.0575
DOT (n = 13)	0.0401	0.0474	0	0.1809
VA (n = 13)	2.5408	0.5340	1.8583	3.7008
EPA (n = 13)	0.1408	0.0590	0.0618	0.2359
NASA (n = 13)	14.0227	1.1590	11.5281	15.7440

Source: Table 3.4.
Key:
USDA: U.S. Department of Agriculture
DOC: Department of Commerce
DOD: Department of Defense
DOE: Department of Energy
HHS: Health and Human Services
DHS: Department of Homeland Security
DOI: Department of Interior
DOT: Department of Transportation
VA: Department of Veterans Affairs
EPA: Environmental Protection Agency
NASA: National Aeronautics and Space Administration

The regression results in Table 3.6 suggest that the ratio of *Invention Disclosures to 100 STEM Employees* has, on average, remained flat over FY 2003 through FY 2015, thus, *for now* (my emphasis), one might reasonably continue to question the general relevance of the process that I have described in terms of the *Experiences → Inventive Ideas* paradigm for federal laboratories/agencies.

Table 3.6   *Regression results from equation (3.2), dependent variable is Invention Disclosures per 100 STEM Employees (standard errors in parentheses)*

Independent Variable	Regression Coefficient
Year	-0.0285
	(0.0351)
USDA	0.2222
	(0.7812)
DOC	-0.3109
	(0.7602)
DOD	9.5728***
	(0.7802)
DOE	34.4195***
	(0.7810)
HHS	2.7583***
	(0.7811)
DOI	-0.4170
	(0.7811)
DOT	-0.3489
	(0.7811)
VA	2.1418***
	(0.7845)
EPA	-0.2696
	(0.7811)
NASA	13.6566***
	(0.7811)
Intercept	57.5968
	(70.6757)
N	139
R^2	0.9855

Notes:
*** significant at .01 level.
The Department of Homeland Security (DHS) is subsumed in the intercept term.
Autocorrelation corrections were done using the Yule-Walker method. My implicit assumption is that the autoregressive pattern in the error terms is constant across agencies.

NOTES

1. Some writers now use the acronym STEAM, where the *A* refers to Arts. Other writers use the acronym STEMM, where the second *M* refers to Medicine.
2. The paper by Link and Van Hasselt (2019) uses STEM employee data in the context of a knowledge production function for the agencies considered in

this book; these authors measured knowledge in terms of the number of patent applications.

3. As an aside, many researchers who study aspects of technology-based behavior hold constant in their empirical analyses the size of the economic unit as measured by the total number of employees. Here, I am offering a more nuanced interpretation of what it means to hold constant, in a statistical analysis, the number of employees in the economic unit. When one holds constant the number of employees as a catchall for the size of the economic unit being studied, I offer the thought that one is, at least in part, holding constant the experience base of the economic unit. See Romer (1990) for a discussion of the myriad elements of human capital.

4. My thanks to John Scott for reminding me that often a laboratory will pursue licenses before the patent is even issued.

5. The Bayh-Dole Act of 1980 (formally the University and Small Business Patent Procedure Act of 1980, Public Law 96-517) legislated behavior for universities that was similar to the legislated behavior for federal laboratories in the Stevenson-Wydler Act of 1980. A detailed description of the Bayh-Dole Act is in Leyden and Link (2015).

6. I emphasize that I am using employees working in the United States because the source for these data (see the source details for Table 3.1) also gives the count of STEM employees for an agency who are working for the agency outside of the United States.

7. See http://www.notable-quotes.com/q/questions_quotes.html (accessed August 3, 2020).

4. Leveraging the experiences to inventive ideas process

R&D BUDGETS

To address the question that I posed at the end of Chapter 3 – namely: Why are the laboratories in some agencies more effective in the *Experiences* → *Inventive Ideas* process than in other agencies? – I consider in this chapter the other resources for which the scientists and researchers in laboratories in all agencies have access to leverage their inventive endeavors. Recall from Chapter 1 that I posited inventive ideas to be functionally related to the stock of human capital (*HC*) and the stock of technical capital (*TC*): *Inventive Ideas* = *f (HC, TC)*. In this chapter, I suggest that the stock of technical capital in a given fiscal year can be measured in terms of an agency's R&D budget in that same fiscal year.[1]

Table 4.1 shows the constant dollar R&D budget ($2019) of each agency by fiscal year; Figures 4.1 through 4.11 show the trend pattern of those R&D budgets over fiscal years.

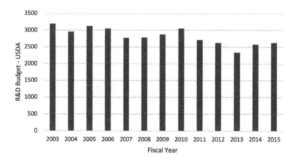

Figure 4.1   *R&D budgets (millions $2019) at the U.S. Department of Agriculture (USDA) by fiscal year, FY 2003–FY 2015*

Table 4.1   R&D budgets (millions $2019) by agency and by fiscal year, FY 2003–FY 2015

Agency	FY 2003	FY 2004	FY 2005	FY 2006	FY 2007	FY 2008	FY 2009	FY 2010	FY 2011	FY 2012	FY 2013	FY 2014	FY 2015
USDA	3 192	2 957	3 123	3 051	2 771	2 783	2 875	3 054	2 712	2 623	2 338	2 580	2 629
DOC	1 631	1 490	1 448	1 329	1 307	1417	1 638	1 564	1 396	1 411	1 433	1 682	1 635
DOD	80 788	87 749	90 731	92 946	96 230	96856	96 124	96 963	90 720	83 798	72 426	72 097	71 253
DOE	11 518	11 593	11 130	10 740	11 004	11657	12 152	12 674	12 239	12 167	11 829	13 002	15 407
HHS	37 735	37 949	37 665	36 253	36 077	34904	36 639	37 144	35 758	35 310	32 933	33 248	32 322
DHS	–	–	–	–	1 213	1187	1 293	1 037	872	541	756	1119	984
DOI	876	834	802	800	788	815	828	908	868	923	868	911	925
DOT	953	884	913	1 023	934	1044	1 091	1 255	1 094	1 035	904	864	950
VA	1 113	1 152	958	963	998	1057	1 112	1 209	1 330	1 305	1 286	1 194	1 262
EPA	773	881	828	778	678	653	664	698	667	639	585	583	558
NASA	14 553	14 375	13 710	14 131	14 106	13345	10 367	10 833	10 434	12 734	12 154	12 742	12 224

Note: R&D budgets are in millions of constant dollars ($2019).
Source: American Association for the Advancement of Science, https://www.aaas.org/programs/r-d-budget-and-policy/historical-trends-federal-rd# (accessed August 3, 2020).
Key:
USDA: U.S. Department of Agriculture
DOC: Department of Commerce
DOD: Department of Defense
DOE: Department of Energy
HHS: Health and Human Services
DHS: Department of Homeland Security
DOI: Department of Interior
DOT: Department of Transportation
VA: Department of Veterans Affairs
EPA: Environmental Protection Agency
NASA: National Aeronautics and Space Administration

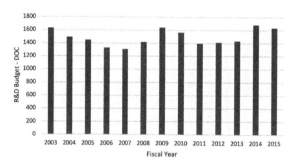

Figure 4.2   *R&D budgets (millions $2019) at the Department of Commerce (DOC) by fiscal year, FY 2003–FY 2015*

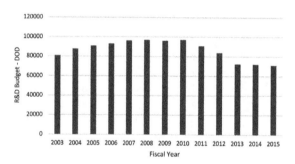

Figure 4.3   *R&D budgets (millions $2019) at the Department of Defense (DOD) by fiscal year, FY 2003–FY 2015*

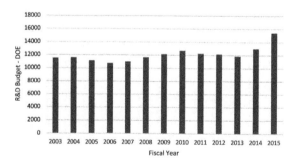

Figure 4.4   *R&D budgets (millions $2019) at the Department of Energy (DOE) by fiscal year, FY 2003–FY 2015*

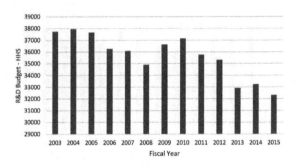

Figure 4.5   *R&D budgets (millions $2019) at Health and Human*
                  Services (HHS) by fiscal year, FY 2003–FY 2015

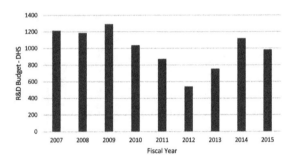

Figure 4.6   *R&D budgets (millions $2019) at the Department of*
                  Homeland Security (DHS) by fiscal year, FY 2007–FY 2015

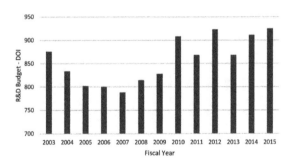

Figure 4.7   *R&D budgets (millions $2019) at the Department of Interior*
                  (DOI) by fiscal year, FY 2003–FY 2015

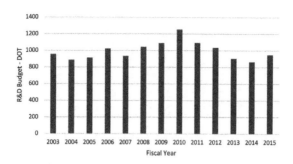

Figure 4.8   *R&D budgets (millions $2019) at the Department of Transportation (DOT) by fiscal year, FY 2003–FY 2015*

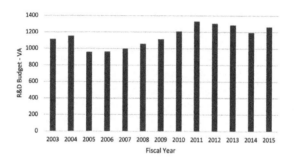

Figure 4.9   *R&D budgets (millions $2019) at the Department of Veterans Affairs (VA) by fiscal year, FY 2003–FY 2015*

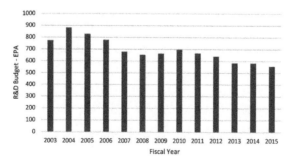

Figure 4.10   *R&D budgets (millions $2019) at the Environmental Protection Agency (EPA) by fiscal year, FY 2003–FY 2015*

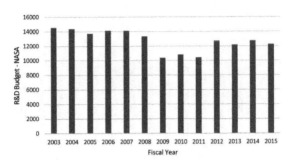

Figure 4.11   R&D budgets (millions $2019) at the National Aeronautics and Space Administration (NASA) by fiscal year, FY 2003– FY 2015

The visual trend pattern in constant dollar R&D budgets from Figures 4.1 through 4.11 is mixed across agencies. For example, the trend pattern is strongly decreasing at Health and Human Services (Figure 4.5) and at the Environmental Protection Agency (Figure 4.10). The trend pattern is mildly decreasing at the U.S. Department of Agriculture (Figure 4.1) and it is mildly increasing and then decreasing at the Department of Defense (Figure 4.3). The trend pattern has been increasing in recent years at the Department of Interior (Figure 4.7) and at the Department of Veterans Affairs (Figure 4.9). In the other agencies, the trend pattern in constant dollar R&D budgets is sporadic.

As in the previous chapters, I consider the trend pattern in R&D budgets more formally through the following regression model:

$$R\&D\ Budgets = \alpha + \beta 4\ Year + Agency\ Controls + \varepsilon \qquad (4.1)$$

Descriptive statistics on *R&D Budgets* by agency are presented in Table 4.2, and the regression results from equation (4.1) are in Table 4.3.

Table 4.2   Descriptive statistics for R&D Budgets (millions $2019) in equation (4.1)

Agency (observations)	Mean	Standard Deviation	Minimum	Maximum
USDA (n = 13)	2 822.15	248.44	2 338	3 192
DOC (n = 13)	1 490.85	125.82	1 307	1 682
DOD (n = 13)	86 821.62	9 829.44	71 253	96 963
DOE (n = 13)	12 085.54	1 188.85	10 740	15 407
HHS (n = 13)	35 687.46	1 878.42	32 322	37 949
DHS (n = 9)	1 000.22	242.02	541	1 293

Agency (observations)	Mean	Standard Deviation	Minimum	Maximum
DOI (n = 13)	857.38	49.39	788	925
DOT (n = 13)	995.69	109.31	864	1 255
VA (n = 13)	1 149.15	128.87	958	1 330
EPA (n = 13)	691.15	98.07	558	881
NASA (n = 13)	12 746.77	1 479.37	10 367	14 553

Source: Table 4.1.
Key:
USDA: U.S. Department of Agriculture
DOC: Department of Commerce
DOD: Department of Defense
DOE: Department of Energy
HHS: Health and Human Services
DHS: Department of Homeland Security
DOI: Department of Interior
DOT: Department of Transportation
VA: Department of Veterans Affairs
EPA: Environmental Protection Agency
NASA: National Aeronautics and Space Administration

Table 4.3   *Regression results from equation (4.1), dependent variable is R&D Budgets (standard errors in parentheses)*

Independent Variable	Regression Coefficient
Year	-109.7619** (48.6427)
USDA	1 234 (1 753)
DOC	836.2311 (1 468)
DOD	80 201*** (1 675)
DOE	13 530*** (1 725)
HHS	32 889*** (1 742)
DOI	-1 404 (1 738)
DOT	-1 283 (1 741)
VA	-1 069 (1 853)
EPA	-2 054 (1 742)
NASA	11 681*** (1 744)

Table 4.3   *Regression results from equation (4.1), dependent variable is*
(continued)   *R&D Budgets (standard errors in parentheses)*

Independent Variable	Regression Coefficient
Intercept	222 535**
	(99 030)
N	139
R^2	0.9960

Notes:
*** significant at .01 level, ** significant at .05 level.
The Department of Homeland Security (DHS) is subsumed in the intercept term.
Autocorrelation corrections were done using the Yule-Walker method. My implicit assumption is
that the autoregressive pattern in the error terms is constant across agencies.
Key:
USDA: U.S. Department of Agriculture
DOC: Department of Commerce
DOD: Department of Defense
DOE: Department of Energy
HHS: Health and Human Services
DHS: Department of Homeland Security
DOI: Department of Interior
DOT: Department of Transportation
VA: Department of Veterans Affairs
EPA: Environmental Protection Agency
NASA: National Aeronautics and Space Administration

The regression results in Table 4.3 suggest that R&D budgets have been slightly decreasing over the fiscal years FY 2003 through FY 2015. On average, the decrease was about $110 million per fiscal year.

THE LEVERAGING EFFECT OF R&D

If it is the case that R&D budgets are positively related to the effectiveness of the *Experiences → Inventive Ideas* process, as measured here in terms of the ratio of *Invention Disclosures to 100 STEM Employees*, then R&D budgets also become a viable target variable for policy makers to help to ensure that the process going from invention disclosures, that is, inventive ideas, to patent applications is both more efficient and more effective (again, see Figure 2.2).

Going from patent applications to patents issued is, in large part, an institutional phenomenon. That transition involves external factors such as the institutional processes within the U.S. Patent and Trademark Office (USPTO). And going to patents issued to an agency receiving royalties or fees from its licensed patented technologies involves both agency supply elements and market demand elements. The market demand side is generally associated with the cyclical nature of the private sector's market for new technology, which also might vary by industry. Public policy has a longer arm when it comes to influencing the timing of patent applications to patents issued than it has on influencing the market demand for new technology, be it new technology from federal laboratories or elsewhere.

To quantify the relationship between R&D budgets in federal agencies and the STEM employees to invention disclosures process, I consider the following regression model:

$$\textit{Invention Disclosures per 100 STEM Employees} = \alpha + \beta 5 \textit{ R\&D per}$$
$$100 \textit{ STEM Employees + Agency Controls} + \varepsilon \qquad (4.2)$$

Descriptive statistics on the ratio of *Invention Disclosures to 100 STEM Employees* were already presented in Chapter 3 in Tables 3.4 and 3.5, and descriptive statistics on the ratio of *R&D to 100 STEM Employees* by agency and by fiscal year are presented in this chapter in Tables 4.2 and 4.3, respectively. Figures 3.12 through 3.22 showed the trend pattern in *Invention Disclosures per 100 STEM Employees* by agency by fiscal year. The trend pattern in *R&D per 100 STEM Employees* by agency by fiscal year is shown in Figures 4.12 through 4.22.

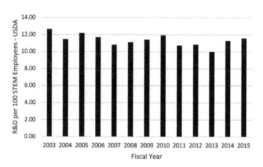

Figure 4.12   *R&D per 100 STEM employees at the U.S. Department of Agriculture (USDA) by fiscal year, FY 2003–FY 2015*

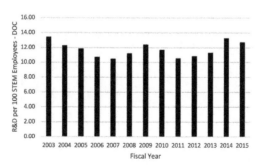

Figure 4.13   *R&D per 100 STEM employees at the Department of Commerce (DOC) by fiscal year, FY 2003–FY 2015*

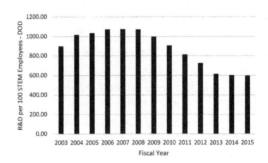

Figure 4.14   *R&D per 100 STEM employees at the Department of Defense (DOD) by fiscal year, FY 2003–FY 2015*

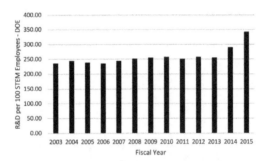

Figure 4.15   *R&D per 100 STEM employees at the Department of Energy (DOE) by fiscal year, FY 2003–FY 2015*

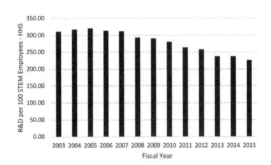

Figure 4.16   *R&D per 100 STEM employees at Health and Human Services (HHS) by fiscal year, FY 2003–FY 2015*

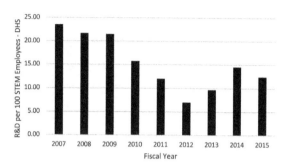

Figure 4.17   *R&D per 100 STEM employees at the Department of Homeland Security (DHS) by fiscal year, FY 2007–FY 2015*

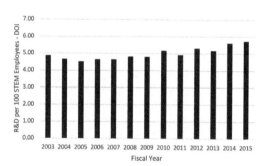

Figure 4.18   *R&D per 100 STEM employees at the Department of Interior (DOI) by fiscal year, FY 2003–FY 2015*

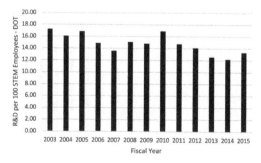

Figure 4.19   *R&D per 100 STEM employees at the Department of Transportation (DOT) by fiscal year, FY 2003–FY 2015*

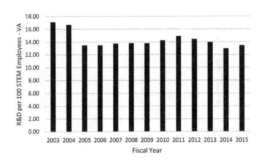

Figure 4.20   *R&D per 100 STEM employees at the Department of*
                    Veterans Affairs (VA) by fiscal year, FY 2003–FY 2015

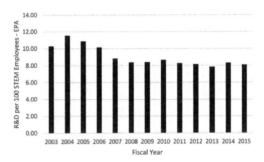

Figure 4.21   *R&D per 100 STEM employees at the Environmental*
                    Protection Agency (EPA) by fiscal year, FY 2003–FY 2015

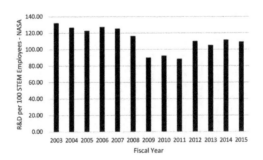

Figure 4.22   *R&D per 100 STEM employees at the National Aeronautics and*
                    Space Administration (NASA) by fiscal year, FY 2003–FY 2015

Regarding trend patterns in *R&D per 100 STEM Employees*, these figures generally show a downward trend pattern since about FY 2005 or so. This is the visual case for the Department of Defense (Figure 4.14), Health and Human Services (Figure 4.16), the Department of Homeland Security (Figure 4.17), and the Environmental Protection Agency (Figure 4.21). There has been a very slight increase in the trend pattern in *R&D per 100 STEM Employees* at the Department of Energy (Figure 4.15), especially in the most recent years, and at the Department of Interior (Figure 4.18). The trend pattern in the other agencies is sporadic.

Descriptive statistics for *R&D per 100 STEM Employees* are presented in Table 4.4, and the regression results from equation (4.2) are presented in Table 4.5. The estimated coefficient on *R&D per 100 STEM Employees*, β_5, is positive, and it is statistically significant. The value of the estimated coefficient is 0.007456, which is interpreted to mean that on average a $100 million increase in *R&D per 100 STEM Employees* is associated with nearly an increase of about 1 *Invention Disclosures per 100 STEM Employees*.

Table 4.4   *Descriptive statistics for R&D per 100 STEM Employees in equation (4.2)*

Agency (observations)	Mean	Standard Deviation	Minimum	Maximum
USDA (n = 13)	11.36	0.69	9.99	12.65
DOC (n = 13)	11.76	1.01	10.47	13.46
DOD (n = 13)	878.55	188.36	597.01	1073.76
DOE (n = 13)	258.39	28.88	235.42	342.30
HHS (n = 13)	281.58	33.63	225.85	319.98
DHS (n = 9)	15.34	5.77	7.01	23.49
DOI (n = 13)	4.99	0.38	4.52	5.74
DOT (n = 13)	14.80	1.63	12.19	17.21
VA (n = 13)	14.31	1.25	12.98	17.10
EPA (n = 13)	9.05	1.22	7.83	11.55
NASA (n = 13)	111.99	14.93	88.27	132.10

Source: Table 3.1 and Table 4.1.
Key:
USDA: U.S. Department of Agriculture
DOC: Department of Commerce
DOD: Department of Defense
DOE: Department of Energy
HHS: Health and Human Services
DHS: Department of Homeland Security
DOI: Department of Interior
DOT: Department of Transportation
VA: Department of Veterans Affairs
EPA: Environmental Protection Agency
NASA: National Aeronautics and Space Administration

Table 4.5   *Regression results from equation (4.2), dependent variable is Invention Disclosures per 100 STEM Employees (standard errors in parentheses)*

Independent Variable	Regression Coefficient
R&D per 100 STEM Employees	0.007456***
	(0.0021)
USDA	0.3230
	(0.5992)
DOC	0.0099
	(0.6012)
DOD	2.8963
	(2.8963)
DOE	32.6218***
	(0.7864)
HHS	0.8110
	(0.8203)
DOI	-0.2173
	(0.5996)
DOT	-0.2821
	(0.5991)
VA	2.1995***
	(0.5993)
EPA	-0.1365
	(0.5993)
NASA	12.9487***
	(0.6327)
Constant	0.2121
	(0.4628)
n	139
R^2	0.9866

Notes:
*** significant at .01 level.
The Department of Homeland Security (DHS) is subsumed in the intercept term.
Autocorrelation corrections were done using the Yule-Walker method. My implicit assumption is that the autoregressive pattern in the error terms is constant across agencies.
Key:
USDA: U.S. Department of Agriculture
DOC: Department of Commerce
DOD: Department of Defense
DOE: Department of Energy
HHS: Health and Human Services
DHS: Department of Homeland Security
DOI: Department of Interior
DOT: Department of Transportation
VA: Department of Veterans Affairs
EPA: Environmental Protection Agency
NASA: National Aeronautics and Space Administration

New inventive ideas do not come cheaply on a per capita basis! That commentary aside, the regression results in Table 4.4 do identify a composite policy target variable that is associated with inventive ideas, namely the amount of R&D associated with the experiences base of researchers and scientists, namely with *R&D per 100 STEM Employees*.

WHAT NEXT?

With reference to Figure 2.2 in Chapter 2, which illustrates that invention disclosures are the driver of patent applications, my next step is to show empirically and statistically that specific relationship. My interpretation of the empirical analyses in this chapter is that, holding constant the number of STEM employees, R&D expenditures drive invention disclosures: *R&D → Invention Disclosures*. This relationship is the implied precursor to all of the elements in Figure 2.2. In Chapter 5, I will show the relationship of (and I am imposing a contemporaneous time dimension) *Invention Disclosures → Patent Applications*, holding constant STEM employees. Thus, conceptually (and I am again imposing a contemporaneous time dimension): *R&D → Invention Disclosures → Patent Applications.*[2]

In Chapter 1, I played devil's advocate when I presented the framework for this book, and I wrote there that a reader might say: "What's the big deal! All that has been shown ... is that an intermediate step has been added to an already defined body of research." In other words, the relevant academic and policy literatures have already developed a framework that models *R&D → Patent Applications*, but I contend that is simply not the most accurate representation of the stages in the technology transfer process in federal laboratories that lead to patent applications. I responded in Chapter 1 to my own rhetorical statement with the following statement: "That individual would be correct ... absolutely correct." But, to reiterate, in my view, the intermediate step is an important one, and it is one that has been overlooked in the relevant literatures. The recognition of the role of invention disclosures in the process leading to patent applications is indeed an important contribution because it underscores not only that investments in laboratory R&D lead to inventive ideas, as reflected in invention disclosures, but also, at a higher level of discussion, it is inventive ideas that are the driver of patent applications and hence the driver of potential new technology entering the economy through licensed patents. Of course, for my point of view to have legs to stand on, I must first demonstrate that *Invention Disclosures → Patent Applications*, and I do that in the following Chapter 5.

NOTES

1. Because the data that I am studying in this book are in the public domain, I leave it to other researchers to aggregate, and perhaps depreciate, annual R&D expenditures over several previous years to construct a weighted stock of technical capital in a current year.
2. The data studied in this book are limited, and thus a detailed investigation of relevant lags is not possible.

5. Inventive ideas as a driver of technology transfer

In this chapter, I offer observational evidence about inventive ideas leading to patent applications, that is, *Inventive Ideas → Patent Applications*. I represented this culmination process in Chapter 1 in equation (1.3), and then it was again represented in Figure 2.2 in terms of the technology transfer process in a federal laboratory. Thus:

$$\text{Patent Applications} = G \ (\text{Inventive Ideas}) \qquad (5.1)$$

where *Patent Applications* obviously refers to patent applications and where *Inventive Ideas* refers to invention disclosures. The operational version of equation (5.1) that I estimate in this chapter is:

$$\text{Patent Applications per 100 STEM Employees} = \alpha + \beta 6 \ \text{Invention}$$
$$\text{Disclosures per 100 STEM Employees} + \text{Agency Controls} + \varepsilon \qquad (5.2)$$

where the independent variables and error term have been previously defined.

Table 5.1 shows *Patent Applications* by agency by fiscal year; Figures 5.1 through 5.11 show the trend pattern in patent applications over time by agency. From the figures, the number of patent applications has generally been increasing over the period FY 2003 through FY 2015 at the U.S. Department of Agriculture (Figure 5.1), the Department of Commerce (Figure 5.2), the Department of Defense (Figure 5.3), and, to a mild extent, at the Department of Energy (Figure 5.4). The trend pattern in the number of patent applications is sporadic at the other agencies.

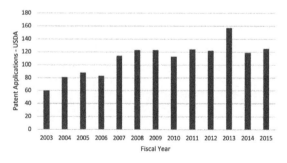

Figure 5.1   *Patent applications at the U.S. Department of Agriculture (USDA) by fiscal year, FY 2003–FY 2015*

Table 5.1   *Patent applications by agency and by fiscal year, FY 2003–FY 2015*

Agency	FY 2003	FY 2004	FY 2005	FY 2006	FY 2007	FY 2008	FY 2009	FY 2010	FY 2011	FY 2012	FY 2013	FY 2014	FY 2015
USDA	60	81	88	83	114	123	123	113	124	122	157	119	125
DOC	5	12	12	5	8	21	20	20	17	25	26	25	30
DOD	810	517	354	691	597	590	690	436	844	1013	942	916	884
DOE	866	661	812	726	693	904	775	965	868	780	944	1144	949
HHS	279	216	230	166	261	164	284	291	272	233	230	216	222
DHS	–	–	–	–	0	0	2	2	12	10	4	5	7
DOI	8	6	3	2	5	7	8	7	2	3	8	4	8
DOT	0	2	5	3	2	2	2	2	2	1	5	0	5
VA	36	54	26	27	25	13	37	13	29	37	25	29	26
EPA	23	12	13	13	15	6	3	3	8	10	7	9	4
NASA	231	207	209	142	127	122	141	150	128	130	150	140	129

Source: Technology Partnerships Office at NIST, https://www.nist.gov/tpo/reports-and-publications (accessed August 3, 2020).

Key:
USDA: U.S. Department of Agriculture
DOC: Department of Commerce
DOD: Department of Defense
DOE: Department of Energy
HHS: Health and Human Services
DHS: Department of Homeland Security
DOI: Department of Interior
DOT: Department of Transportation
VA: Department of Veterans Affairs
EPA: Environmental Protection Agency
NASA: National Aeronautics and Space Administration

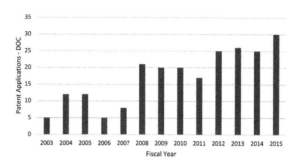

Figure 5.2   *Patent applications at the Department of Commerce (DOC) by fiscal year, FY 2003–FY 2015*

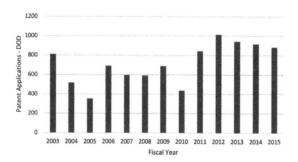

Figure 5.3   *Patent applications at the Department of Defense (DOD) by fiscal year, FY 2003–FY 2015*

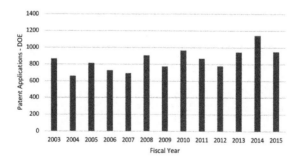

Figure 5.4   *Patent applications at the Department of Energy (DOE) by fiscal year, FY 2003–FY 2015*

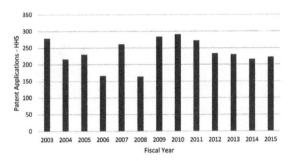

Figure 5.5   *Patent applications at Health and Human Services (HHS) by fiscal year, FY 2003–FY 2015*

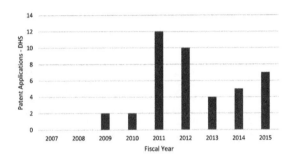

Figure 5.6   *Patent applications at the Department of Homeland Security (DHS) by fiscal year, FY 2007–FY 2015*

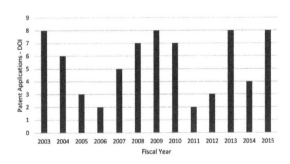

Figure 5.7   *Patent applications at the Department of Interior (DOI) by fiscal year, FY 2003–FY 2015*

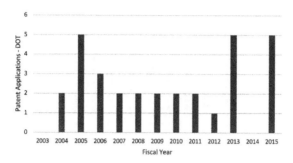

Figure 5.8   *Patent applications at the Department of Transportation (DOT) by fiscal year, FY 2003–FY 2015*

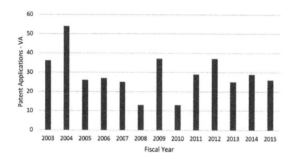

Figure 5.9   *Patent applications at the Department of Veterans Affairs (VA) by fiscal year, FY 2003–FY 2015*

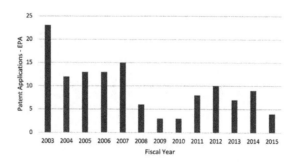

Figure 5.10   *Patent applications at the Environmental Protection Agency (EPA) by fiscal year, FY 2003–FY 2015*

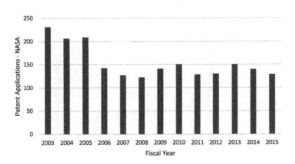

*Figure 5.11   Patent applications at the National Aeronautics and Space
             Administration (NASA) by fiscal year, FY 2003–FY 2015*

Table 5.2 shows *Patent Applications per 100 STEM Employees* by agency
by fiscal year; Figures 5.12 through 5.22 show *Patent Applications per 100
STEM Employees* over time by agency. From the figures, the following
generalizations are possible. The per capita (i.e., per 100 STEM employees)
trend pattern in patent applications remains positive at the U.S. Department of
Agriculture (Figure 5.12) and at the Department of Commerce (Figure 5.13)
as was the case with *Patent Applications* in Figures 5.1 and 5.2. The trend
pattern in *Patent Applications per 100 STEM Employees* is negative at Health
and Human Services (Figure 5.16), at the Department of Veterans Affairs
(Figure 5.20), at the Environmental Protection Agency (Figure 5.21), and at
the National Aeronautics and Space Administration (Figure 5.22). The trend
pattern is sporadic at the other agencies.

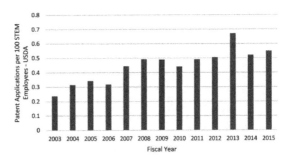

*Figure 5.12   Patent Applications per 100 STEM Employees at the U.S.
             Department of Agriculture (USDA) by fiscal Year, FY 2003–
             FY 2015*

Table 5.2   Patent applications per 100 STEM employees by agency and by fiscal year, FY 2003–FY 2015

Agency	FY 2003	FY 2004	FY 2005	FY 2006	FY 2007	FY 2008	FY 2009	FY 2010	FY 2011	FY 2012	FY 2013	FY 2014	FY 2015
USDA	0.238	0.313	0.343	0.318	0.445	0.491	0.489	0.441	0.491	0.504	0.671	0.520	0.550
DOC	0.041	0.099	0.098	0.040	0.064	0.166	0.152	0.150	0.129	0.192	0.205	0.197	0.234
DOD	9.01	5.993	4.037	7.977	6.662	6.525	7.158	4.074	7.555	8.755	8.011	7.628	7.407
DOE	17.746	13.925	17.413	15.914	15.393	19.508	16.271	19.582	17.798	16.487	20.393	25.559	21.084
HHS	2.299	1.805	1.954	1.436	2.256	1.377	2.250	2.197	2.008	1.704	1.659	1.544	1.551
DHS	–	–	–	–	0	0	0.033	0.030	0.165	0.130	0.051	0.065	0.089
DOI	0.044	0.033	0.017	0.012	0.030	0.041	0.046	0.040	0.011	0.017	0.048	0.025	0.050
DOT	0	0.036	0.092	0.044	0.029	0.029	0.027	0.027	0.027	0.014	0.070	0	0.070
VA	0.553	0.782	0.366	0.378	0.345	0.170	0.458	0.153	0.325	0.409	0.271	0.315	0.278
EPA	0.306	0.157	0.171	0.170	0.195	0.077	0.038	0.037	0.099	0.127	0.094	0.128	0.060
NASA	2.097	1.823	1.871	1.278	1.130	1.062	1.220	1.277	1.083	1.121	1.297	1.225	1.150

Source: Based on the data in Table 5.1 and Table 3.1.

Key:
USDA: U.S. Department of Agriculture
DOC: Department of Commerce
DOD: Department of Defense
DOE: Department of Energy
HHS: Health and Human Services
DHS: Department of Homeland Security
DOI: Department of Interior
DOT: Department of Transportation
VA: Department of Veterans Affairs
EPA: Environmental Protection Agency
NASA: National Aeronautics and Space Administration

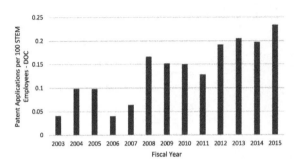

Figure 5.13　　　*Patent applications per 100 STEM employees at the Department of Commerce (DOC) by fiscal year, FY 2003–FY 2015*

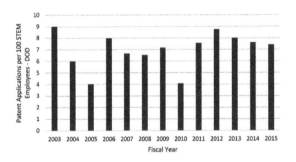

Figure 5.14　　　*Patent applications per 100 STEM employees at the Department of Defense (DOD) by fiscal year, FY 2003– FY 2015*

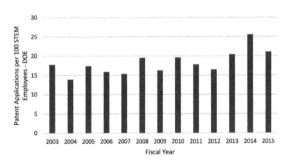

Figure 5.15　　　*Patent applications per 100 STEM employees at the Department of Energy (DOE) by fiscal year, FY 2003–FY 2015*

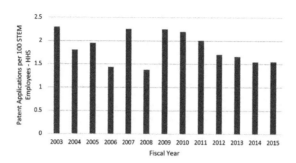

*Figure 5.16   Patent applications per 100 STEM employees at Health and
Human Services (HHS) by fiscal year, FY 2003–FY 2015*

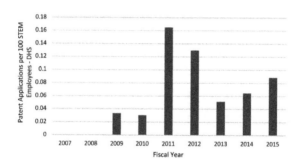

*Figure 5.17   Patent applications per 100 STEM employees at the Department
of Homeland Security (DHS) by fiscal year, FY 2007–FY 2015*

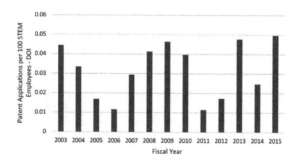

*Figure 5.18   Patent applications per 100 STEM employees at the
Department of Interior (DOI) by fiscal year, FY 2003–FY 2015*

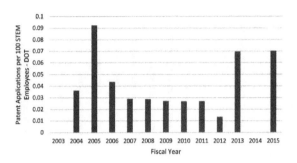

Figure 5.19   Patent applications per 100 STEM employees at the Department of Transportation (DOT) by fiscal year, FY 2003–FY 2015

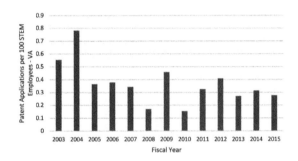

Figure 5.20   Patent applications per 100 STEM employees at the Department of Veterans Affairs (VA) by fiscal year, FY 2003–FY 2015

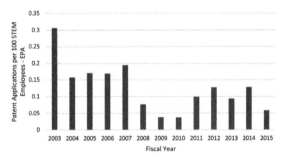

Figure 5.21   Patent applications per 100 STEM employees at the Environmental Protection Agency (EPA) by fiscal year, FY 2003–FY 2015

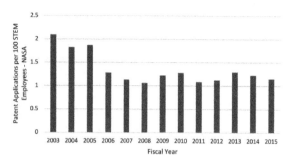

Figure 5.22   *Patent applications per 100 STEM employees at the National Aeronautics and Space Administration (NASA) by fiscal year, FY 2003–FY 2015*

With reference to equation (5.2), descriptive statistics on *Patent Applications per 100 STEM Employees* by agency are in Table 5.3. Recall that descriptive statistics on *Invention Disclosures per 100 STEM Employees* were presented in Table 3.4. And, the regression results from the estimation of equation (5.2) are in Table 5.4.

Table 5.3   *Descriptive statistics for Patent Applications per 100 STEM Employees in equation (5.2)*

Agency (observations)	Mean	Standard Deviation	Minimum	Maximum
USDA (n = 13)	0.4474	0.1169	0.2378	0.6710
DOC (n = 13)	0.1360	0.0637	0.0404	0.2337
DOD (n = 13)	6.9837	1.5455	4.0374	9.0070
DOE (n = 13)	18.2364	3.0263	13.9246	25.5585
HHS (n = 13)	1.8493	0.3316	1.3771	2.2988
DHS (n = 9)	0.0626	0.0565	0	0.1652
DOI (n = 13)	0.0319	0.0142	0.0113	0.0496
DOT (n = 13)	0.0358	0.0273	0	0.0923
VA (n = 13)	0.3695	0.1642	0.1532	0.7820
EPA (n = 13)	0.1275	0.0745	0.0371	0.3060
NASA (n = 13)	1.3564	0.3407	1.0623	2.0968

Source: Table 3.1 and Table 5.2.
Key:
USDA: U.S. Department of Agriculture
DOC: Department of Commerce
DOD: Department of Defense
DOE: Department of Energy
HHS: Health and Human Services
DHS: Department of Homeland Security
DOI: Department of Interior
DOT: Department of Transportation
VA: Department of Veterans Affairs
EPA: Environmental Protection Agency
NASA: National Aeronautics and Space Administration

Table 5.4   *Regression results from equation (5.2), dependent variable is Patent Applications per 100 STEM Employees (standard errors in parentheses)*

Independent Variable	Regression Coefficient
Invention Disclosures per 100 STEM Employees	0.1700** (0.0678)
USDA	0.3343 (0.5729)
DOC	0.0369 (0.5599)
DOD	5.3973*** (0.8659)
DOE	12.3848*** (2.4054)
HHS	1.2883** (0.6036)
DOI	-0.0760 (0.5730)
DOT	0.0089 (0.5729)
VA	-0.0699 (0.5930)
EPA	0.0833 (0.5727)
NASA	-1.0000 (1.0918)
Constant	0.0095 (0.4389)
N	139
R^2	0.9695

Notes:
*** significant at .01 level, ** significant at .05 level.
The Department of Homeland Security (DHS) is subsumed in the intercept term.
Autocorrelation corrections were done using the Yule-Walker method. My implicit assumption is that the autoregressive pattern in the error terms is constant across agencies.
Key:
USDA: U.S. Department of Agriculture
DOC: Department of Commerce
DOD: Department of Defense
DOE: Department of Energy
HHS: Health and Human Services
DHS: Department of Homeland Security
DOI: Department of Interior
DOT: Department of Transportation
VA: Department of Veterans Affairs
EPA: Environmental Protection Agency
NASA: National Aeronautics and Space Administration

The estimated regression coefficient on *Disclosures per 100 STEM Employees*, *β6*, in Table 5.4 is positive and significantly different from zero. That coefficient is interpreted to mean that on average a 10 unit increase in *Invention Disclosures per 100 STEM Employees* is associated with an increase of 1.7 *Patent Applications per 100 STEM Employees*.

Thus, reflecting on the regression results from Tables 4.5 and 5.4, we can offer the following generalizations. From Table 4.5, a $100 million increase in *R&D per 100 STEM Employees* is associated with an increase of nearly 1 (i.e., 0.75) *Invention Disclosures per 100 STEM Employees*. Or, a $1,333.3 million increase in *R&D per 100 STEM Employees* is associated with an increase of 10 *Invention Disclosures per 100 STEM Employees*. And, from Table 5.4, an increase of 10 *Invention Disclosures per 100 STEM Employees* is associated with an increase of 1.7 *Patent Applications per 100 STEM Employees*. Without invoking a causal relationship, and speaking in per capita (in 100s) terms, one might generalize that on average a new patent application from a U.S. federal laboratory is associated with an outlay of about $784 million as a result of the relationship between R&D expenditures, invention disclosures, and patent applications.

If one ignores the *R&D → Invention Disclosures* relationship, as the extant literature on the knowledge production functions has, for the most part,[1] and if one only examines a model with *Patent Applications per 100 STEM Employees* as the dependent variable and *R&D per 100 STEM Employees* as the independent variable (along with agency fixed effects), one would have found that the regression coefficient on *R&D per 100 STEM Employees* was not significantly different from zero, and one might conclude that agency R&D budgets are not an effective direct policy target variable for enhancing technology transfer from federal laboratories. However, agency R&D budgets are indeed an effective policy target variable when consideration is given to R&D budgets being related to invention disclosures *and* (my emphasis) invention disclosures then being related to patent applications. I will revisit this concluding observation in Chapter 8.

I now take a bit of a detour, and I offer an observation as to (perhaps) why one should not think about a *R&D → Patent Applications* relationship at all. I am not advocating this position because of the statistical insignificance that I report just above from a regression between *Patent Applications per 100 STEM Employees* and *R&D per 100 STEM Employees*, for an inspection of the references in this book will show that I have been involved in my share of published studies of public sector knowledge production functions using data related to federal laboratories. And, in those studies I considered empirical models of federal laboratory patent applications that are functionally related to federal laboratory R&D budgets. I am taking this detour to briefly present a public policy perspective about how federal R&D (perhaps) should be allocated, and then to suggest an alternative perspective, based on the analyses in this book, on how one might think of allocating federal R&D differently.

Robert Atkinson, in a lucid and influential 2019 report from his Information Technology and Innovation Foundation (ITIF), offers an observation about how the public sector can boost U.S. productivity through investments in R&D. He writes (Atkinson, 2019, pp. 10–12):

> To make scientific and engineering research a stronger tool for driving productivity growth, the federal government needs to do two main things. The first is to spur an increase in government and business R&D. The second is to better allocate that R&D to areas most likely to spur productivity growth. This will require recognizing productivity-related innovation as a key national mission that deserves support from government the same way defense, health, and energy do. And it will require recognizing that the allocation of that funding cannot be determined solely on the basis of the interests of individual scientists, but rather should be based more on societal interests, as determined by government … If we are to better boost productivity through research, the *federal government* [my emphasis] needs to allocate the next marginal dollar on areas that have the biggest impact on economic growth. The first step in that process would be to recognize that some federally supported research is much more likely than others to impact growth.

I do not disagree with this observation, but perhaps, in light of the analyses described in this book, one might think in somewhat different terms. I mention these different terms based on a reflection on the ideas I discussed in previous chapters. I simply summarize my thoughts as: scientific ideas beget scientific ideas.

I am not sure how one knows a priori how to identify or how "to allocate the next marginal dollar on areas that have the biggest impact on economic growth." How would one know where the "biggest impact on economic growth" would occur; would that underlying technology necessarily be on the upward sloping portion of its life cycle or would the underlying technology already be on the tailing off portion of its life cycle?[2] Might a better policy prescription, albeit one for which measurable outcomes will be slower—actually much slower—to observe, be to allocate the marginal R&D dollar to scientists and researchers in federal laboratories to develop and then to disclose their new scientific ideas? What policy makers would be doing is to allocate the marginal R&D dollar to basic research rather than applied research and development, and there is a rich literature that suggests the marginal rate of return to public sector investments in basic research far exceeds the marginal rate of return to public sector investments in applied research and development (Link, 1981).

NOTES

1. The paper by Link, Morris, and Van Hasselt (2019) is a notable exception.
2. Some of the technologies that Atkinson (2019) defines are, from my vantage, on the upward sloping portion of their life cycle, but not all policy makers, with their constituent-driven agenda, are so astute. Atkinson identifies robotics, autonomous transportation systems, artificial intelligence, additive manufacturing, material sciences, microelectronics and advanced computing, and life sciences. It should be noted that some of these technology areas are the same as those identified by the Technology Administration within the Department of Commerce, based on data and information relative to the mid to late 1980s, in which the United States was behind in international markets (DOC, 1990). This point is discussed again in Chapter 6.

6. Inventive ideas as a driver of technology transfer activity: a case study

In this chapter, I replicate the analysis of Chapter 5 using data specific to one federal laboratory: the National Institute of Standards and Technology (NIST) within the Department of Commerce. But first, I offer a brief history of NIST in the following section of this chapter to provide context for the NIST data as the illustrative units of analysis. Recall, too, that all of the data presented in this book come from the Technology Partnerships Office at NIST.

NATIONAL INSTITUTE OF STANDARDS AND TECHNOLOGY (NIST)

The history of NIST, the national metrology laboratory in the United States, begins with the passage of the March 3, 1901 Act (Public Law 177-56), often referred to as the Organic Act of 1901. This legislation created the National Bureau of Standards (NBS) within the Department of the Treasury from the existing Office of Standard Weights and Measures. Then, in late 1901, the Bureau was transferred from the Department of the Treasury to the newly established Department of Commerce and Labor.

The Organic Act states:

> That the functions of the [B]ureau shall consist in the custody of the standards; the comparison of the standards used in scientific investigations, engineering, manufacturing, commerce, and educational institutions with the standards adopted or recognized by the Government; the construction, when necessary, of standards, their multiples and subdivisions; the testing and calibration of standard measuring apparatus; the solution of problems which arise in connection with standards; the determination of physical constants and the properties of materials, when such data are of great importance to scientific or manufacturing interests and are not to be obtained of sufficient accuracy elsewhere.

I have previously written (Link, 2019) that the Organic Act of 1901, and the activities of the Bureau, might reasonably be viewed as the first national effort to legislate the transfer of technology in the form of technical knowledge from the public sector to organizations throughout the economy.[1]

World War I brought about an understanding of the need for standardization across agencies that purchased goods that are supply chain related. Thus, the transfer of technology—tacit technical knowledge in the form of know-how as well as codified practices—from the public sector's Bureau to private sector manufacturers had begun, and it increased exponentially during the first decade of the Bureau's life (Cochrane, 1966).

During World War II, the Bureau focused on the development and improvement of military technology. And, by the end of World War II, there was growing opinion that the federal government, through the expertise of the Bureau, should be responsible for basic research—the discovery of new knowledge—rather than continue to pursue an applied industrial research agenda. However, the basic research versus applied research debate continued until an ad hoc study committee of the National Academy of Sciences recommended that the Bureau be restored to its "essential services for our industrial society" (Cochrane, 1966, p. 496). The ad hoc committee also made a recommendation for the modernization of the Bureau's facilities, which needed to be rebuilt, and ground was broken on June 14, 1961 on a 550-acre plot of land in Gaithersburg, Maryland. The Gaithersburg campus was dedicated in 1966.

As Schooley (2000, p. 646) suggests:

> Given the increased emphasis on international competitiveness, technology transfer, and industrial productivity in the dialog between NBS and Congress during the 1980s, new legislation to re-define the mission of the Bureau was almost a certainty. The change in the name of the agency—in the view of the Congress—merely served to underscore its new role within the Department of Commerce.

It was a well-known fact by the mid to late 1970s that many U.S. industries were faltering in terms of their technological advances. For example, total factor productivity (TFP) is widely regarded as an index of technological advancement within an economy. See Chapter 2. I have written extensively about the culprits for the productivity slowdown shown in Figure 2.1 with Don Siegel and my colleague Dennis Leyden (e.g., Link and Siegel, 2003; Leyden and Link, 2015), but many other scholars also point to declining investments in R&D spending as a culprit for the slowdown in technological advancements, which, in turn, was detrimental to productivity growth. Causation aside, one consequence of these slowdown periods was a decline in the international competitiveness of many industries in the United States.[2]

In fact, the Technology Administration within the Department of Commerce reported, based on data and information relative to the mid to late 1980s, several emerging technologies in which the trend was that the United States was losing, and in some instances losing badly, in international markets relative to Japan, in particular (DOC, 1990, p. 13):

- The United States was losing in terms of trends in R&D investments in advanced materials, biotechnology, digital imaging technology, sensor technology, and superconductors.
- The United States was losing in terms of trends in new product introductions in advanced materials, advanced semiconductor devices, high-density data storage, high-performance computing, medical devices and diagnostics (including digital imaging technology), optoelectronics, and superconductors.

In the mid 1980s, Congress considered "several initiatives to improve American competitiveness in world-wide markets" (Schooley, 2000, p. 613). These considerations were finally codified in the Omnibus Trade and Completeness Act of 1988 (Public Law 100-418). Stated therein:[3]

> The National Bureau of Standards since its establishment has served as the Federal focal point in developing basic measurement standards and related technologies, has taken a lead role in stimulating cooperative work among private industrial organizations in efforts to surmount technological hurdles, and otherwise has been responsible for assisting in the improvement of industrial technology ... It is the purpose of this Act to rename the National Bureau of Standards as the National Institute of Standards and Technology [NIST] and to modernize and restructure that agency to augment its unique *ability to enhance the competitiveness of American industry* [my emphasis] ... The Secretary of Commerce ... acting through the Director of the Institute ... and, if appropriate, through other officials, is authorized to take all actions necessary and appropriate to accomplish the purposes of this Act, including the following functions of the Institute ... to invent, develop, and (when appropriate) promote *transfer to the private sector* [my emphasis] of measurement devices to serve special national needs ... to demonstrate the results of the Institute's activities by exhibits or other *methods of technology transfer* [my emphasis], including the use of scientific or technical personnel of the Institute for part-time or intermittent teaching and training activities at educational institutions of higher learning as part of and incidental to their official duties ...

ANALYSIS OF NIST DATA

In this chapter, I demonstrate empirically the relationship that underlies the technology transfer process in a federal laboratory as shown in Figure 2.2. In particular, the analyses presented below confirm the *R&D → Invention Disclosure → Patent Applications* relationship already demonstrated in the previous chapters to hold when using laboratory aggregated data by agency area studies.

For these confirmation analyses, I estimate each of the equations that have been estimated in previous chapters, but I only use NIST data. The NIST data cover the period of FY 2000 through FY 2018, and they come from the NIST annual reports to the Technology Partnerships Office. R&D budgets and the number of STEM employees come from the same sources as the data in the previous chapters. See the source details for Table 6.1.

Table 6.1   *NIST data used to estimate equations (6.1) and (6.2), FY 2000–FY 2018*

FY	Invention Disclosures	Patent Applications	R&D Budget	STEM Employees
2000	32	18	679.6	1460
2001	24	9	582.2	1431
2002	16	11	697.8	1661
2003	16	5	670.3	1711
2004	23	8	607.6	1620
2005	19	5	573.9	1618
2006	10	4	546	1625
2007	29	6	592.9	1647
2008	40	18	618.1	1653
2009	36	19	652.2	1761
2010	30	19	687.5	1780
2011	25	17	610.4	1728
2012	52	24	626.9	1765
2013	33	23	658.7	1751
2014	41	21	710	1850
2015	46	26	716.5	1961
2016	46	21	808.4	2046
2017	40	43	781.6	2054
2018	71	54	992.4	2048

Sources:
Invention Disclosures and Patent Applications: Technology Partnerships Office, https://www.nist.gov/tpo/reports-and-publications/reports (accessed August 3, 2020).
R&D Budget: American Association for the Advancement of Science, https://www.aaas.org/programs/r-d-budget-and-policy/historical-trends-federal-rd# (accessed August 3, 2020).
STEM Employees: Office of Personnel Management, https://www.fedscope.opm.gov/employment.asp (accessed September 3, 2020).

Table 6.2   *Descriptive statistics on the variables in equations (6.1) and (6.2), n = 19*

Variable	Mean	Standard Deviation	Minimum	Maximum
Invention Disclosures per 100 STEM Employees	1.86	0.7015	0.6154	3.4668
R&D per 100 STEM Employees	38.60	3.7263	33.6000	48.4570
Patent Applications per 100 STEM Employees	1.018	0.6125	0.2462	2.6367

Table 6.3   *Regression results from equation (6.1), dependent variable is Invention Disclosures per 100 STEM Employees (standard errors in parentheses)*

Independent Variable	Regression Coefficient
R&D per 100 STEM Employees	0.0963**
	(0.0415)
Constant	-1.8457
	(1.6485)
n	19
R^2	0.3643

Notes:
** significant at .05 level.
Autocorrelation corrections were done using the Yule-Walker method.

Table 6.4   *Regression results from equation (6.2), dependent variable is Patent Applications per 100 STEM Employees (standard errors in parentheses)*

Independent Variable	Regression Coefficient
Invention Disclosures per 100 STEM Employees	0.6783***
	(0.1323)
Constant	-0.2440
	(0.2643)
N	19
R^2	0.6442

Notes:
*** significant at .01 level.
Autocorrelation corrections were done using the Yule-Walker method.

The first equation, equation (6.1), parallels equation (4.2) from Chapter 4; the second equation, equation (6.2), parallels equation (5.2) from Chapter 5.[4] Specifically:

$$Invention\ Disclosures\ per\ 100\ STEM\ Employees = \alpha + \beta 7\ R\&D\ per\ 100\ STEM\ Employees + \varepsilon \qquad (6.1)$$

and

$$Patent\ Applications\ per\ 100\ STEM\ Employees = \alpha + \beta 8\ Invention\ Disclosures\ per\ 100\ STEM\ Employees + \varepsilon \qquad (6.2)$$

Descriptive statistics on the three focal variables in equations (6.1) and (6.2) are in Table 6.2. The regression results from equations (6.1) and (6.2) are in Tables 6.3 and 6.4, respectively.

The regression results from equation (6.1), which are presented in Table 6.3, are interpreted as follows. The estimated coefficient on *R&D per 100 STEM Employees*, *β7*, is positive, and it is statistically different from zero. The value of the estimated coefficient is 0.0963, and it is interpreted to mean that on average a $100 million increase in *R&D per 100 STEM Employees* is associated with an increase of nearly 10 *Invention Disclosures per 100 STEM Employees*. In Chapter 4, my interpretation of the empirical findings from the regression estimates from equation (4.2) using the agency data were: "The value of the estimated coefficient is 0.007456, which is interpreted to mean that on average a $100 million increase in *R&D per 100 STEM Employees* is associated with nearly an increase of 1 *Invention Disclosures per 100 STEM Employees*." The invention disclosures responsiveness of NIST scientists and researchers to an increase in R&D funding is, literally, 10 times greater. Although the agency data used to estimate equation (4.2) include Department of Commerce information, and NIST is a Department of Commerce laboratory, there are other agencies that are, shall we say, pulling down the invention disclosures responsiveness of scientists and researchers to increases in R&D. If I may generalize from this simple and limited comparison of empirical results, with all the usual caveats being implicit, one might conclude that across the board increases in R&D funding will have differential invention disclosures effects at the agency level, and it might also be the case that within an agency there will be similar differential effects.

To return to Chapter 5, I quoted from Robert Atkinson (Atkinson, 2019, pp. 11–12):

> If we are to better boost productivity through research, the *federal government* [my emphasis] needs to allocate the next marginal dollar on areas that have the biggest impact on economic growth. The first step in that process would be to recognize that some federally supported research is much more likely than others to impact growth.

Atkinson is absolutely correct that there will be differential impacts on economic growth from a marginal R&D dollar, just as I have shown with respect to the impact of R&D on invention disclosures at NIST.

The regression results from equation (6.2), which are presented in Table 6.4, are interpreted as follows. The estimated coefficient on *Disclosures per 100 STEM Employees*, $\beta 8$, is positive and statistically different from zero. The value of the estimated coefficient is 0.6783, and it is interpreted to mean that on average a 10 unit increase in *Invention Disclosures per 100 STEM Employees* is associated with an increase of 6.8 *Patent Applications per 100 STEM Employees*. In Chapter 5, my interpretation of the empirical findings from the regression estimates from equation (5.2) using the agency data were: "The estimated regression coefficient on *Disclosures per 100 STEM Employees* [is 0.1700]. That coefficient is interpreted to mean that on average a 10 unit increase in *Invention Disclosures per 100 STEM Employees* is associated with an increase of 1.7 *Patent Applications per 100 STEM Employees*." Again, NIST's patent application process is more responsive to changes in invention disclosures than are the federal agencies as a group.

To conclude, for the NIST federal laboratory, *R&D per 100 STEM Employees* is also a relevant policy target variable associated with technology transfer activity through patent applications that lead to licensable technologies. Perhaps future laboratory focused case studies will confirm this conclusion. And perhaps future laboratory case studies will document inter-laboratory intra-agency differences on the impact associated with R&D investments.

NOTES

1. A more detailed history of NIST is available in Link (2019) and Link and Oliver (2020). Portions of this section of this chapter draw directly from those two sources.
2. There were a number of Congressional responses to this productivity slowdown, as discussed in Chapter 2, but the scope of motivation for several legislative initiatives was broader than the productivity slowdown. For example, as stated in the Joint Research and Development Act of 1984: "Joint research and development as our foreign competitors have learned [Japan] can be pro-competitive. It can reduce duplication, promote the efficient use of scarce technical personnel, and help to achieve desirable economies of scale [in R&D]."
3. The section (Subtitle B, Part I) of the Omnibus Trade and Competitiveness Act from which this excerpt about the National Bureau of Standards and the National Institute of Standards and Technology is quoted is called the Technology Competitiveness Act.
4. No fixed effects controls are included in these models because all of the data come from one federal laboratory: NIST.

7. CRADAs: market failure and government failure?

As I discussed in Chapter 2, one might interpret the use of public moneys to support R&D in federal laboratories as a public sector response to a market failure. That is, the private sector was not investing a sufficient amount of R&D to develop the new technologies that will possibly be licensed to other organizations in the public and private sectors. This underinvestment may be the result of specialized markets (i.e., small markets) for the technologies that come from research in federal laboratories, needed production economies of scale that many firms could not achieve, and/or the risk associated with commercializing in which such markets is greater than the level associated with private sector hurdle rates.[1] According to Tassey (2020, p. x):

> A major barrier to these needed investments [in R&D] is the fact that companies apply significant discount factors when considering R&D investments. Underinvestment can therefore result from (1) a significant degree of technical and market risk that characterize most early-phase technology platform research, (2) the propensity of technical knowledge to leak, and (3) the long time typically needed to reach the point of commercialization. These factors explain why industrialized nations promote various forms of cooperative research to pool risk, capture economies of scope, and reduce the average time to completion of the R&D stage, thereby enabling scale-up to commercial production levels and subsequent market penetration.

In this chapter, I present the concept of government failure in response to a market failure, and I argue that the government failure concept is *not* (my emphasis) a relevant interpretation of the following relationship: *R&D → Patent Disclosures → CRADAs* for which the *Patent Disclosures → CRADAs* relationship is not statistically significant.

COOPERATIVE RESEARCH AND DEVELOPMENT AGREEMENTS (CRADAS)

The so-called mirepoix of technology transfer mechanisms relevant to federal laboratories consists of patents, licenses, and CRADAs. In the previous chapters, I have focused on patent applications, a precursor to patents awarded, and licensing royalties from the applied for and awarded patents. My focus on patent applications was motivated by the technology transfer diagram in Figure 2.2 and the fact that patent applications are a so-called "go versus no go" decision within the TTO of a federal laboratory. In contrast, patents awarded are confounded by legislation that affects the USPTO as well as the internal activities (e.g., review times) of the USPTO.[2] Licensing revenues are confounded by the cyclical nature of the market demand for new technologies. Here, I focus on CRADAs, although they too are confounded by the demand of third parties for collaborative research with a federal laboratory, which are permitted by legislation, but they are a widely recognized technology transfer mechanism.

What are CRADAs?[3] To enhance the technology transfer mission of federal laboratories, Congress amended the Stevenson-Wydler Act of 1980 in October 1986 with the passage of the Federal Technology Transfer Act of 1986 (Public Law 99-502).[4] The 1986 Act states:

> Each Federal agency may permit the director of any of its Government-operated Federal laboratories to enter into cooperative research and development agreements [CRADAs] on behalf of such agency with other Federal agencies; units of State or local government; industrial organizations (including corporations, schools and partnerships, and limited partnerships, and industrial development organizations); public and private foundations; nonprofit organizations (including universities); or other persons (including licensees of inventions owned by the Federal agency); and to negotiate licensing agreements ... for Government-owned inventions made at the laboratory and other inventions of Federal employees that may be voluntarily assigned to the Government.

A CRADA is, according to the Federal Technology Transfer Act of 1986:

> any agreement between one or more Federal laboratories and one or more non-Federal parties under which the Government, through its laboratories, provides personnel, services, facilities, equipment, or other resources with or without reimbursement (but not funds to non-Federal parties) and the non-Federal parties provide funds, personnel, services, facilities, equipment, or other resources toward the conduct of specified research or development efforts which are consistent with the missions of the laboratory ...

And CRADAs are important as discussed in the Federal Laboratory Consortium for Technology Transfer's *Technology Transfer Desk Reference: A Comprehensive Guide to Technology Transfer* (FLC, 2013, pp. 33–6):

> [CRADAs] ... provide federal laboratories with an extremely flexible vehicle to facilitate the transfer of commercially useful technologies from federal laboratories to the nonfederal sector ... The establishment of cooperative R&D efforts through a CRADA has perhaps the greatest possibility for long-term payoff of any technology transfer mechanism. An intimate working relationship between federal and

commercial researchers will allow the federal side to understand commercial needs and allow ideas from the commercial sector to flow into federal laboratories.

Recall my earlier discussion in Chapter 5 about the logic of the $R\&D \rightarrow$ *Invention Disclosures* $\rightarrow$ *Patent Applications* relationships. They follow directly from Figure 2.2. Now consider the following $R\&D \rightarrow$ *Invention Disclosures* $\rightarrow$ *CRADAs* relationship as an extension of Figure 2.2. My emphasis on this extension is motivated, in part, by the fact that CRADAs are an important technology transfer mechanism (Link, Oliver, Jordan, and Hayter, 2019; Link and Oliver, 2020) and that they were in fact signaled out as an important technology transfer mechanism in President Obama's 2011 Memorandum. This relationship can be quantified as:

$$CRADAs \; per \; 100 \; STEM \; Employees = \alpha + \beta 9 \; Invention \; Disclosures$$
$$per \; 100 \; STEM \; Employees + Agency \; Controls + \varepsilon \qquad (7.1)$$

Data on CRADAs are in Table 7.1, by agency and by fiscal year; descriptive statistics on *CRADAs per 100 STEM Employees* are in Table 7.2, and the regression results from equation (7.1) are in Table 7.3. As shown in Table 7.3, the regression coefficient on *Invention Disclosures per 100 STEM Employees* is positive, but it is not significantly different from zero.

GOVERNMENT FAILURE

A discussion of government failure, in certain circumstances, goes hand in hand with a discussion of market failure. Winston (2006, pp. 2–3) writes:[5]

> Government failure, then, arises when government has created inefficiencies because it should not have intervened in the first place or when it could have solved a given problem or set of problems more efficiently, that is, by generating greater net benefits.

Winston (2006, p. 3) also notes:

> From a policy perspective, market failure should be a matter of concern when market performance significantly deviates from the appropriate efficiency benchmark. Similarly, a government failure should call a government intervention into question when economic welfare is actually reduced or when resources are allocated in a manner that significantly deviates from an appropriate efficiency benchmark.

My analysis of CRADAS above parallels the analysis of patent applications that I presented in Chapters 5 and 6. My motivation for focusing on CRADAS, as I have previously mentioned, is, in part, based on the fact that CRADAS are a well-established and often studied (e.g., Chen, Link, and Oliver, 2018) technology transfer mechanism. My other motivation for focusing on CRADAS

Table 7.1   CRADAs by agency and by fiscal year, FY 2003–FY 2015

Agency	FY 2003	FY 2004	FY 2005	FY 2006	FY 2007	FY 2008	FY 2009	FY 2010	FY 2011	FY 2012	FY 2013	FY 2014	FY 2015
USDA	55	44	55	57	69	77	81	92	102	65	86	60	80
DOC	1767	1790	1764	2158	1865	1585	1512	2159	2192	2844	2289	2111	2548
DOD	630	768	679	705	641	745	659	720	762	757	769	671	793
DOE	140	157	164	168	182	178	176	176	178	184	142	180	184
HHS	102	95	101	66	68	83	105	83	81	93	104	98	112
DHS	–	–	–	–	–	8	6	14	31	53	76	88	98
DOI	12	16	21	38	112	98	74	82	295	284	376	423	586
DOT	7	0	5	6	7	6	7	0	8	12	8	10	9
VA	8	4	3	26	52	155	438	491	450	522	453	505	509
EPA	39	23	33	16	18	49	83	33	26	22	51	35	23
NASA	0	0	1	0	0	0	1	0	0	0	0	0	0

Source: Technology Partnerships Office at NIST, https://www.nist.gov/tpo/reports-and-publications (accessed August 3, 2020).
Key:
USDA: U.S. Department of Agriculture
DOC: Department of Commerce
DOD: Department of Defense
DOE: Department of Energy
HHS: Health and Human Services
DHS: Department of Homeland Security
DOI: Department of Interior
DOT: Department of Transportation
VA: Department of Veterans Affairs
EPA: Environmental Protection Agency
NASA: National Aeronautics and Space Administration

Table 7.2   Descriptive statistics for CRADAs per 100 STEM Employees in equation (7.1)

Agency (observations)	Mean	Standard Deviation	Minimum	Maximum
USDA (n = 13)	0.2872	0.0711	0.1705	0.4036
DOC (n = 13)	16.1080	2.8217	11.4606	21.8450
DOD (n = 13)	7.1448	0.8866	5.5875	8.9023
DOE (n = 13)	3.6340	0.3728	2.8689	4.0880
HHS (n = 13)	0.7168	0.1009	0.5710	0.8580
DHS (n = 8)	0.6158	0.4602	0.0997	1.2386
DOI (n = 13)	1.1095	1.1462	0.0667	3.6352
DOT (n = 13)	0.0954	0.0478	0	0.1634
VA (n = 13)	3.1687	2.5772	0.0422	5.7854
EPA (n = 13)	0.4535	0.2303	0.2088	1.0468
NASA (n = 13)	0.0014	0.0033	0	0.0090

Source: Technology Partnerships Office at NIST, https://www.nist.gov/tpo/reports-and -publications (accessed August 3, 2020) and Table 3.1.
Key: USDA: U.S. Department of Agriculture
DOC: Department of Commerce
DOD: Department of Defense
DOE: Department of Energy
HHS: Health and Human Services
DHS: Department of Homeland Security
DOI: Department of Interior
DOT: Department of Transportation
VA: Department of Veterans Affairs
EPA: Environmental Protection Agency
NASA: National Aeronautics and Space Administration

is because, in a statistical sense, such activities are not directly dependent on invention disclosures as were patent applications.[6] My point is that the *Invention Disclosures → Patent Applications* relationship cannot be generalized to all technology transfer mechanisms.

The fact that there is not statistical support for an *Inventions Disclosures → CRADAs* relationship should not be interpreted as evidence of government failure. On the contrary. One reason for the lack of statistical support for the relationship is that CRADA activity involves at least two research parties and external legislative initiatives. One research party is within the federal laboratory and the other research party is not. The other research party, say a private sector firm, is driven to engage in CRADA activity with a federal laboratory because of a number of factors including the firm's internal inability to conduct all of the R&D it needs, as well as the external market demand for the firm needing a technology within a federal laboratory to remain competitive in the market place or to gain a competitive advantage. Legislative initiatives can influence the willingness of either party to engage in CRADA-based research.

Table 7.3 *Regression results from equation (7.1), dependent variable is CRADAs per 100 STEM Employees (standard errors in parentheses)*

Independent Variable	Regression Coefficient
Invention Disclosures per 100 STEM Employees	0.0435
	(0.0685)
USDA	-0.4377
	(0.8785)
DOC	15.2616***
	(0.7935)
DOD	5.0609***
	(1.1210)
DOE	1.1159
	(2.5356)
HHS	-0.5069
	(0.9016)
DOI	0.1014
	(0.8777)
DOT	-1.4170
	(0.8777)
VA	1.6472*
	(0.9040)
EPA	-0.7629
	(0.8777)
NASA	
Constant	1.1316*
	(0.6823)
	-1.6684
	(1.2952)
n	138
R^2	0.9590

Notes:
*** significant at .01 level, * significant at .10 level.
The Department of Homeland Security (DHS) is subsumed in the intercept term.
Autocorrelation corrections were done using the Yule-Walker method. My implicit assumption is that the autoregressive pattern in the error terms is constant across agencies.

NOTES

1. Atkinson (2019, pp. 8–9) presents the market failure argument very well: "Some argue that increases in federal spending on scientific and engineering research are not needed because the private sector can be relied on to adequately invest and drive innovation. There are two reasons why this is not correct. The first relates to spillovers from business-funded research wherein businesses invest less than what are societally optimal levels because they cannot capture all of the returns … The second relates to the fact that government research often 'crowds in' business research, leading firms to invest more than they would otherwise, thus increasing productivity and economic welfare."
2. See, for example, Cohen (2004) and Hall (2004).
3. Chen, Link, and Oliver (2018) recently reviewed the relevant literature on CRADAs. See Feldman (1990), Sink and Easley (1994), Wu (1994), Bozeman and Papadakis (1995), Prosser (1995), Ham and Mowery (1995, 1998), Mowery (2003), and Franza, Grant, and Spivey (2012).
4. The Federal Technology Transfer Act of 1986 made clear that Government Owned, Government Operated laboratories (GOGOs) could enter into CRADAs, but the Act was not specific about Government Owned, Contractor Operated laboratories (GOCOs). See Link and Oliver (2020) for a more detailed discussion of GOGO laboratories and GOCO laboratories.
5. See also le Grand (1991).
6. A topic that has not been studied is the relationship between invention disclosures and CRADAs. The argument might be that invention disclosures are a prerequisite for scientists and researchers in a federal laboratory having the state of the art knowledge to attract private sector organizations to partner with the federal laboratory scientists and researchers and with their internal technologies.

8.   Concluding observations

REFLECTING ON THE SET STAGE

In Chapter 1, I quoted from both President Obama's October 2011 Presidential Memorandum and President Trump's *The President's Management Agenda* in an effort to highlight the national importance of federal R&D, especially federal R&D allocations to the transfer of technology from federal laboratories. *The President's Management Agenda* deserves greater attention than I gave it in Chapter 1 not only because it arguably builds on President Obama's Presidential Memorandum, which in my view invigorated a long overdue discussion about technology transfer from federal laboratories, but also because *The President's Management Agenda* contains more technology initiative specifics than were even included even in President George H.W. Bush's *U.S. Technology Policy* in 1990 (Executive Office of the President, 1990). Arguably, *U.S. Technology Policy* was the first formal statement of U.S. technology policy, although I accept the argument that a U.S. technology policy is embedded in Vannevar Bush's (no relationship) *Science—the Endless Frontier* (Bush, 1945).[1]

The President's Management Agenda suggests 14 Cross Agency Priority (CAP) Goals that relate to a "long-term vision for effective and modern government capabilities that work on behalf of the American people" (Trump, undated, p. 7). Of particular relevance to the topics of this book is CAP Goal 14: Improve Transfer of Federally Funded Technologies from Lab-to-Market.

That Goal is (p. 47): "Improve the transfer of technology from federally funded research and development to the private sector to promote U.S. economic growth and national security."

The challenge of this goal is stated in *The President's Management Agenda* as (p. 47):

> The Federal Government invests approximately $150 billion annually in research and development (R&D) conducted at Federal laboratories, universities, and other research organizations … [I]t is essential to optimize technology transfer and support programs to increase the return on investment (ROI) from federally funded R&D.

The Goal will (p. 47):[2,3]

> Improve the transition of federally funded innovations from the laboratory to the marketplace ... [d]evelop and implement more effective partnering models and technology transfer mechanisms for Federal agencies; and [e]nhance the effectiveness of technology transfer by improving the methods for evaluating the ROI and economic and national security impacts of federally funded R&D, and using that information to focus efforts on approaches proven to work.

In Chapter 2, I offered a framework, based on Figure 2.2, as the motivation for the descriptive analysis in this book. It can be represented as: *R&D → Invention Disclosures → Patent Applications → Patent Issues → Patent Licensing.*[4] The fundamental point of this framework is that R&D activity is the starting point for the entire technology transfer process. Federal R&D is the requisite investment that leads to invention disclosures, and with invention disclosures in hand, a laboratory is, shall we say, off to the races. One particular laboratory might not win the race because invention disclosures are a necessary condition for patent licenses not a sufficient condition. Stated differently, creative ideas are not equal and not all creative ideas eventually reach the market.[5]

But, and this is an important qualifying "but," a look at the trend patterns in R&D budgets across federal agencies, that is, at R&D budgets across federal laboratories aggregated to the agency level, as shown in Figures 4.1 through 4.11, gives me pause. There is not a single federal agency represented in those figures for which the trend pattern since 2003 is consistently positive. In fact, across federal agencies, the trend pattern is on average negative as the regression estimates in Table 4.3 show.

In Chapter 3, I posed the *Experiences → Inventive Ideas* concept in an effort to make the case that even though R&D investments are the catalyst for the technology transfer process shown in Figure 2.2, R&D investments simply are *the* (my emphasis) resource-based fuel for inventive individuals (i.e., STEM employees) to ultimately be able to offer inventive ideas to their relevant technology transfer office. Still, the trend pattern in STEM employees has not been consistently positive in any agency since 2003, as shown in Figures 3.1 through 3.11, although in some agencies the trend pattern is positive more often than is the trend pattern in R&D budgets. The fact that there is more of a consistent positive trend in STEM employees over time than in R&D budgets over time explains mathematically why, on average, the trend pattern in *R&D per 100 STEM Employees* is often negative, and when not negative, then that trend pattern is sporadic (see Figures 4.12 through 4.22).

POLICY IMPLICATIONS

The policy implications from this book come in terms of the findings from two regression models. First, I show in Table 4.5 that *R&D per 100 STEM Employees → Invention Disclosures per 100 STEM Employees* is, on average, a statistically significant relationship. This finding is a statistical counterpart to the upper left cell in Figure 2.2, which is reproduced here as Figure 8.1. Then, second, I show in Table 5.4 that *Invention Disclosures per 100 STEM Employees → Patent Applications per 100 STEM Employees* is also a statistically significant relationship. This latter finding documents a critical stage of the technology transfer process described in Figure 8.1.

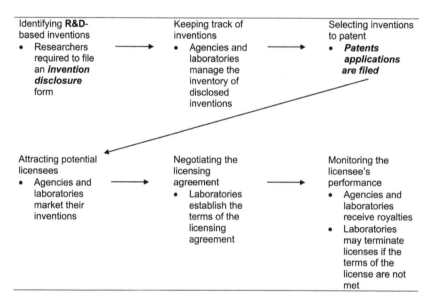

Figure 8.1   *The invention disclosures to patent licensing process*

Source: Based on GAO (2018, p. 11).

Walter G. Copan, the Under Secretary of Commerce for Standards and Technology and Director of the National Institute of Standards and Technology, prefaced NIST Special Publication 1234 *Return on Investment Initiative for*

Unleashing American Innovation with the following statement (NIST, 2018, p. iii):

> The Return on Investment (ROI) Initiative for Unleashing American Innovation is part of a national conversation that is designed to advance the Lab-to-Market Cross Agency Priority (CAP) Goal 14 of the President's Management Agenda (PMA). The ROI Initiative's vision is to unleash American innovation into our economy. The goal is to maximize the transfer of Federal investments in science and technology into value for America in ways that will (a) meet current and future economic and national security needs in a rapidly shifting technology marketplace and enhance U.S. competitiveness globally, and (b) attract greater private sector investment to create innovative products, processes, and services, as well as new businesses and industries.

The underlying argument in the *Return on Investment Initiative*, known as the *Green Paper*, is (NIST, 2018, p. 6):

> U.S. economic competitiveness is strengthened by the ability of private sector-companies to advance the new technologies resulting from basic R&D [in federal laboratories], and to deliver the products and services that drive the Nation's economy forward.

The President's Management Agenda CAP Goal 14 sets forth five strategies for accomplishing Goal 14: "Improve the transfer of technology from federally funded research and development to the private sector to promote U.S. economic growth and national security." These strategies are (Trump, undated, p. 47):

> (1) identify regulatory impediments and administrative improvements in Federal technology transfer policies and practices; (2) increase engagement with private sector technology development experts and investors; (3) build a more entrepreneurial R&D workforce; (4) support innovative tools and services for technology transfer; and (5) improve understanding of global science and technology trends and benchmarks.

The *Return on Investment Initiative* outlines on pages 119 through 122 a policy agenda comprised of 15 intended action items to complement these five strategies. With specific reference to the arguments in this book, and the arguments in this book are narrower than the subject matter in *The President's Management Agenda*, these action items highlight the following.

Regarding strategy (1) above to identify regulatory impediments and administrative improvements in federal technology transfer policies and practices, the *Return on Investment Initiative* states that NIST will (NIST, 2018, p. 120):

> Implement regulatory change under Executive Order 10096; Legislative change is required to codify the Federal employee's requirement to report inventions and assign all right, title, and interest in work related inventions to the Federal Government.

Regarding strategy (3) above to build a more entrepreneurial R&D workforce, the *Return on Investment Initiative* states that the Department of Commerce (DOC) through NIST along with the White House Office of Science and Technology Policy (OSTP) will (NIST, 2018, p. 121):

> Establish a designated job series to recruit, develop, and retain well qualified professionals—with both business and scientific/technical backgrounds—to pursue a career in Federal technology transfer.

My reading of the *Return on Investment Initiative* is that, again with a specific reference to the arguments in this book, there is a policy initiative to improve the invention disclosures process and enhance the experiences resources (i.e., human capital) involved in federal R&D. Again, from the perspective of this book, a policy emphasis on R&D, invention disclosures, and human capital is not only well focused but also a relationship that needs to be emphasized, and in some instances repaired (based on declining trends in invention disclosures).

Greg Tassey, former Chief Economist at NIST, has developed and, over time, refined a model of what he calls the technology development life cycle (Tassey, 2020). It is an in-depth model of the relationships among elements of a nation's technology ecosystem. I discuss this model here because it provides a framework and/or platform to emphasize the importance of scientific ideas being the genesis element and the driving force that enriches many of the other elements of the technology ecosystem.

The Tassey model validates, conceptually, the importance of the findings in this book that scientific ideas, proxied by new invention disclosures, are *a*, if not *the*, critical element of the technology development life cycle, and thus scientific ideas must continue to flourish and be enriched or leveraged through relevant resources such as R&D (*TC* from Chapter 1) and the experiences embodied in the human capital base (*HC* from Chapter 1). My empirical demonstration of the statistical relationship *R&D* → *Invention Disclosures* → *Patent Applications* is, in my view, an initial step toward understanding that R&D is a critical input into scientific ideas (invention disclosures), and scientific ideas are a critical input into steps leading to new technologies entering society (through licensed patented technologies).

Let me place this argument in the context of the Tassey model. At the base of his model is what he calls the Science Base. It represents the reservoir of publicly funded scientific knowledge from universities, federal laboratories, and research institutes. Here, I have focused only on federal laboratories, but below I make a call for research similar to what I have presented here to be done at the university level.

Much like a supply chain for elements of technology development, knowledge from the Science Base has an impact on the development of proprietary technologies, and the development of proprietary technologies has an impact on entrepreneurial ability to bring those technologies to market, that is, to successfully burgeon new innovations.

AGENDA FOR FUTURE RESEARCH

The use of these federal laboratory technology transfer metrics by researchers to extend empirical research on the relevance of a knowledge production function representation of a *R&D → Patent Applications* relationship has in large part been based on the specification of a knowledge production function that has been shown to be relevant to the private sector (e.g., see Link and Van Hasselt, 2019; Link, Morris, and Van Hasselt, 2019; and Link and Oliver, 2020). Herein, I have been in the previous chapters exploring the relevance of such a framework to the public sector.

More specifically, I have in this book illustrated that a *R&D → Patent Application* relationship is an imprecise representation of technology transfer in federal laboratories, and thus the traditionally relied on knowledge production function approach (e.g., see Hall and Ziedonis, 2001; Czarnitzki, Kraft, and Thorwarth, 2009) is perhaps less than appropriate for the study of public sector R&D activity that ultimately leads to patent applications.

There are a number of areas for additional research that can meaningfully expand on the ideas and descriptive analyses that I explored in the previous chapters. From a narrow perspective, but still an important perspective, I have not accounted for time lags in any of the regression models, and that step forward certainly needs to be done in the aggregate or in laboratory-specific case studies. Also, I have explicitly assumed in all of the analyses herein that technical capital in a fiscal year can be represented by contemporaneous R&D investments. Logically, a more realistic representation of technical capital in a given fiscal year might be based on a weighted average of several previous fiscal years of R&D investments.

Shifting focus, one might reasonably explore whether or not there are inter-laboratory or intra-laboratory differences in the demographic characteristics of researchers and scientists who are successful in disclosing an invention and then having that invention selected to be patented.

From a broader perspective, to the best of my knowledge (at the time of writing this book) the knowledge production function concept has yet to be systematically applied to university R&D investments, invention disclosures, and patent applications. Relevant data are available from the Association of University Technology Managers (AUTM), but a challenge will be identifying the relevant stock of technical capital to assign as a prerequisite to an invention disclosure from a member of the university's faculty or staff.

I conclude this book with a quote from the science fiction writer Frank Herbert: "There is no real ending. It's just a place where you stop the story."[6]

NOTES

1. For such an historical perspective, see also Sargent and Shea (2014) and Hart (2014).
2. *The President's Management Agenda* offers with this CAP Goal a figure that shows over the FY 2011 through FY 2015 period an upward sloping trend pattern for patents issued and invention licenses, but a downward sloping trend pattern for invention disclosures. From my own vantage, while I applaud CAP Goal 14, I am puzzled about the absence of a discussion about the implications of a downward sloping trend pattern for invention disclosures. If one is to increase the ROI associated with federal investments in R&D, the relevant comparative metrics are invention licenses, which are inventions that are patented or could be patented and thus licensed, and related licensing royalties. How long will the upward sloping trend for patents issues and invention licenses continue when invention disclosures have been decreasing? I am also puzzled by the fact that R&D budgets to all federal agencies in the aggregate were, in $2019 constant dollars, $158,416 million in 2016, $132,738 million in 2017, and $147,292 million in 2018 (American Association for the Advancement of Science, https://www.aaas.org/programs/r -d-budget-and-policy/historical-trends-federal-rd#, accessed August 3, 2020). As shown in Figure 2.2 and discussed at length in the previous chapters, it is R&D that drives invention disclosures, and it is invention disclosures that ultimately drive patent application and then patents issues.
3. Pressman, Planting, Yuskavage, Bond, and Moylan (2018, p. 6), under the sponsorship of NIST, completed a study of the economic impacts of federal laboratory licensing, the final stage in the technology transfer process in Figures 2.2 and 8.1. Under two alternative sets of assumptions, the authors found: "Under a first set of assumptions called Rev 1, and summing over 8 years of data from 2008–2015, the total contribution of these federal laboratory licensors to industry gross output ranges from $23.1 billion to $76.5 billion in 2009 U.S. dollars; contributions to gross domestic product (GDP) range from $10.6 billion to $34.6 billion in 2009 U.S. dollars. Estimates of the total number of person years of employment supported range from 73,000 to 215,000 over the eight-year period. Under a second set of assumptions called Rev 2, and summing over the same 8 years of data from 2008–2015, the total contribution of these federal laboratory licensors to industry gross output ranges from $25 billion to $83.6 billion in 2009 U.S. dollars; contributions to GDP range from $12.5 billion to $41.3 billion in 2009 U.S. dollars. Estimates of the total number of person years of employment supported range from 86,000 to 265,000 over the eight-year period."

4. There are similar characterizations of the process beside that by the Government Accounting Office (GAO, 2018) from which Figure 2.2 is based. Again, I thank John Scott, as I did in an endnote to Chapter 3, for reminding me that often a laboratory will pursue licenses before the patent is even issued.

5. From my own perspective, I emphasize that the GAO report (GAO, 2018) from where Figures 2.2 and 8.1 are based is titled "FEDERAL RESEARCH: Additional Actions Needed to Improve Licensing of Patented Laboratory Inventions." My hope is that at some point in the near future there will be a second GAO report, perhaps influenced by this book, entitled "FEDERAL RESEARCH: Additional Actions Needed to Increase Invention Disclosures in Federal Laboratories."

6. See https://www.highnote.reviews/category/aspiring-quotes/page/2/ (accessed August 3, 2020).

References

Acemoglu, Daron, Ufuk Akcigit, and William R. Kerr (2016). "Innovation Network," *Proceedings of the National Academy of Sciences*, 113: 11483–8.

Atkinson, Robert D. (2019). "Why Federal R&D Policy Needs to Prioritize Productivity to Drive Growth and Reduce the Debt-to-GDP Ratio," Information Technology and Innovation Foundation Report.

Audretsch, David B. (1998). "Agglomeration and the Location of Innovative Activity," *Oxford Review of Economic Policy*, 14: 18–29.

Audretsch, David B. and Albert N. Link (2019). *Sources of Knowledge and Entrepreneurial Behavior*, Toronto: University of Toronto Press.

Audretsch, David B., Albert N. Link, and Martijn van Hasselt (2019). "Knowledge Begets Knowledge: University Knowledge Spillovers and the Output of Scientific Papers from U.S. Small Business Innovation Research (SBIR) Projects," *Scientometrics*, 121: 1367–83.

Ballard, Pierre-Alexandre, Cristian Jara-Figueroa, Sergio Petralia, Mathieu Steijn, David Rigby, and César A. Hidalgo (2020). "Complex Economic Activities Concentrate in Large Cities," *Nature Human Behavior*, 3: 1–10.

Bozeman, Barry (2000). "Technology Transfer and Public Policy: A Review of Research and Theory," *Research Policy*, 29: 627–55.

Bozeman, Barry and Albert N. Link (2015). "Toward an Assessment of Impacts from U.S. Technology and Innovation Policies," *Science and Public Policy*, 43: 369–76.

Bozeman, Barry and Maria Papadakis (1995). "Company Interactions with Federal Laboratories: What They Do and Why They Do It," *Journal of Technology Transfer*, 20: 64–74.

Burke, James (1978). *Connections*, New York: Simon & Schuster.

Bush, Vannevar (1945). *Science—the Endless Frontier*, Washington, DC: National Science Foundation.

Carter, President Jimmy (1979). "Joint Hearings before the U.S. Senate Committee on Commerce, Science, and Transportation and the Select Committee on Small Business; and to the U.S. House of Representatives Committee on Science and Technology and the Committee on Small Business," Washington, DC: Government Printing Office.

Chen, Chuchu, Albert N. Link, and Zachary T. Oliver (2018). "U.S. Federal Laboratories and Their Research Partners: A Quantitative Case Study," *Scientometrics*, 115: 501–17.

Cochrane, Rexmond C. (1966). *Measures for Progress: A History of the National Bureau of Standards*, Washington, DC: National Bureau of Standards.

Cohen, Wesley M. (2004). "Patents and Appropriation: Concerns and Evidence," *Journal of Technology Transfer*, 30: 57–71.

Czarnitzki, Dirk., K. Kornelius Kraft, and Susanne Thorwarth (2009). "The Knowledge Production of 'R' and 'D'," *Economics Letters*, 105: 141–3.

David, Paul A. (1985). "Clio and the Economics of QWERTY," *American Economic Review*, 75: 332–7.

DOC (U.S. Department of Commerce) (1990). "Emerging Technologies: A Survey of Technical and Economic Opportunities," Washington, DC: Technology Administration.

Executive Office of the President (1990). *U.S. Technology Policy*, Washington, DC: Executive Office of the President.

Feldman, David L. (1990). "Transferring Superconductivity Technology at a National-Laboratory User Center," *Journal of Technology Transfer*, 15: 15–24.

FLC (Federal Laboratory Consortium for Technology Transfer) (2013). *Technology Transfer Desk Reference: A Comprehensive Guide to Technology Transfer*, Cherry Hill, NJ: Federal Laboratory Consortium for Technology Transfer.

FLC (Federal Laboratory Consortium for Technology Transfer) (2017). *Technology Transfer Playbook*, Cherry Hill, NJ: Federal Laboratory Consortium for Technology Transfer.

Franza, Richard M., Kevin P. Grant, and W. Austin Spivey (2012). "Technology Transfer Contracts between R&D Labs and Commercial Partners: Choose Your Words Wisely," *Journal of Technology Transfer*, 37: 577–87.

GAO (United States Government Accounting Office) (2018). "FEDERAL RESEARCH: Additional Actions Needed to Improve Licensing of Patented Laboratory Inventions," Report to the Chairman, Committee on the Judiciary, House of Representatives, GAO-18-327, Washington, DC: Government Accounting Office.

Gertner, Jon (2012). *The Idea Factory: Bell Labs and the Great Age of American Innovation*, New York: Penguin Group.

Glaeser, Edward L., Hedi D. Kallal, Jose A. Scheinkman, and Andrei Shleifer (1992). "Growth in Cities," *Journal of Political Economy*, 100: 1126–52.

Griliches, Zvi (1979). "Issues in Assessing the Contribution of Research and Development to Productivity Growth," *Bell Journal of Economics*, 10: 92–116.

Hall, Bronwyn H. (2004). "Exploring the Patent Explosion," *Journal of Technology Transfer*, 30: 35–48.

Hall, Bronwyn H. and Rosemarie H. Ziedonis (2001). "The Patent Paradox Revisited: An Empirical Study of Patenting in the U.S. Semiconductor Industry, 1979–1995," *RAND Journal of Economics*, 32: 101–28.

Ham, Rosemarie M. and David C. Mowery (1995). "Improving Industry–Government Cooperative R&D," *Issues in Science and Technology*, Summer: 67–73.

Ham, Rosemarie M. and David C. Mowery (1998). "Improving the Effectiveness of Public–Private R&D Collaboration: Case Studies at a U.S. Weapons Laboratory," *Research Policy*, 26: 661–75.

Hart, David M. (2014). "An Agent, Not a Mole: Assessing the White House Office of Science and Technology Policy," *Science and Public Policy*, 41: 411–18.

Hayter, Christopher S., Albert N. Link, and John T. Scott (2018). "Public-Sector Entrepreneurship," *Oxford Review of Economic Policy*, 34: 676–94.

Hébert, Robert F. and Albert N. Link (2009). *A History of Entrepreneurship*, London: Routledge.

Hobbs, Kelsi G., Albert N. Link, and John T. Scott (2017a). "The Growth of US Science and Technology Parks: Does Proximity to a University Matter?" *Annals of Regional Science*, 59: 495–511.

Hobbs, Kelsi G., Albert N. Link, and John T. Scott (2017b). "Science and Technology Parks: An Annotated and Analytical Literature Review," *Journal of Technology Transfer*, 42: 957–76.

Johnson, Steven (2010). *Where Good Ideas Come From: The Natural History of Innovation*, New York: Penguin Group.

le Grand, Julian (1991). "The Theory of Government Failure," *British Journal of Political Science*, 21: 423–42.

Leyden, Dennis P. and Albert N. Link (2015). *Public Sector Entrepreneurship: U.S. Technology and Innovation Policy*, New York: Oxford University Press.

Link, Albert N. (1981). "Basic Research and Productivity Increase in Manufacturing: Additional Evidence," *American Economic Review*, 71: 1111–12.

Link, Albert N. (2019). "Technology Transfer at the US National Institute of Standards and Technology," *Science and Public Policy*, 46: 906–12.

Link, Albert N. (2020). "University Science and Technology Parks: A U.S. Perspective," in S. Amoroso, A. Link, and M. Wright (eds), *Science and Technology Parks and Regional Economic Development*, New York: Palgrave Macmillan, pp. 25–38.

Link, Albert N. and Zachary T. Oliver (2020). *Technology Transfer and U.S. Public Sector Innovation*, Cheltenham, UK and Northampton, MA, USA: Edward Elgar.

Link, Albert N. and Frederic M. Scherer (2005). *Essays in Honor of Edwin Mansfield: The Economics of R&D, Innovation and Technological Change*, New York: Springer.

Link, Albert N. and John T. Scott (2003). "U.S. Science Parks: The Diffusion of an Innovation and Its Effects on the Academic Mission of Universities," *International Journal of Industrial Organization*, 21: 1323–56.

Link, Albert N. and John T. Scott (2006). "U.S. University Research Parks," *Journal of Productivity Analysis*, 25: 43–55.

Link, Albert N. and John T. Scott (2007). "The Economics of University Research Parks," *Oxford Review of Economic Policy*, 23: 661–74.

Link, Albert N. and John T. Scott (2011). *Public Goods, Public Gains: Calculating the Social Benefits of Public R&D*, New York: Oxford University Press.

Link, Albert N. and John T. Scott (2012). *Employment Growth from Public Support of Innovation in Small Firms*, Kalamazoo, MI: W.E. Upjohn Institute for Employment Research.

Link, Albert N. and John T. Scott (2013). *Bending the Arc of Innovation: Public Support of R&D in Small, Entrepreneurial Firms*, New York: Palgrave Macmillan.

Link, Albert N. and John T. Scott (2018). "Geographic Proximity and Science Parks," in the *Oxford Research Encyclopedia of Economics and Finance*, DOI: 10.1093/acrefore/9780190625979.013.272.

Link, Albert N. and Donald S. Siegel (2003). *Technological Change and Economic Performance*, London: Routledge.

Link, Albert N. and Martijn van Hasselt (2019). "A Public Sector Knowledge Production Function," *Economics Letters*, 174: 64–6.

Link, Albert N., Robert S. Danziger, and John T. Scott (2018). "Is the Bayh-Dole Act Stifling Biomedical Innovation?" *ISSUES in Science and Technology*, Winter: 33–5.

Link, Albert N., Cody A. Morris, and Martijn van Hasselt (2019). "The Impact of Public R&D Investments on Patenting Activity: Technology Transfer at the U.S.

Environmental Protection Agency," *Economics of Innovation and New Technology*, 28: 536–46.

Link, Albert N., Zachary T. Oliver, Gretchen B. Jordan, and Christopher Hayter (2019). *Overview and Analysis of Technology Transfer from Federal Agencies and Laboratories*, Report prepared for the National Institute of Standards and Technology by RTI Institute, Research Triangle Park.

Link, Albert N., Donald S. Siegel, and David van Fleet (2011). "Public Science and Public Innovation: Assessing the Relationship between Patenting at U.S. National Laboratories and the Bayh-Dole Act," *Research Policy*, 40: 1094–9.

Locke, John (1996). *An Essay Concerning Human Understanding* (ed. K.P. Winkler), Cambridge, UK: Hackett Publishing Company. Originally published in 1690.

Machlup, Fritz (1980). *Knowledge and Knowledge Production*, Princeton, NJ: Princeton University Press.

Marshall, Alfred (1919). *Industry and Trade*. London: Macmillan.

Mowery, David C. (2003). "Using Cooperative Research and Development Agreements as S&T Indicators: What Do We Have and What Would We Like?" *Technology Analysis and Strategic Management*, 15: 89–205.

National Academy of Sciences, National Academy of Engineering, and Institute of Medicine (2007). *Rising Above the Gathering Storm: Energizing and Employing America for a Brighter Economic Future*, Washington, DC: The National Academies Press.

National Commission on Excellence in Education (1983). *A Nation at Risk: The Imperative for Educational Reform*, Washington, DC: U.S. Department of Education.

NIST (National Institute of Standards and Technology) (2018). *Return on Investment Initiative for Unleashing American Innovation* (also known at the *Green Paper*), Gaithersburg, MD: National Institute of Standards and Technology.

Obama, President Barack (2011). "Presidential Memorandum—Accelerating Technology Transfer and Commercialization of Federal Research in Support of High-Growth Businesses," Washington, DC: The White House, https://www.govinfo.gov/app/details/DCPD-201100803 (accessed August 18, 2020).

Pressman, Lori, Mark Planting, Robert Yuskavage, Jennifer Bond, and Carol Moylan (2018). *A Preliminary Application of an I-O Economic Impact Model to US Federal Laboratory Inventions: 2008–2015*, Gaithersburg, MD: National Institute of Standards and Technology.

Prosser, Glen A. (1995). "The Role of Incentives in the Deployment of Technologies from Cooperative R&D," *Journal of Technology Transfer*, 20: 13–17.

Romer, Paul M. (1990). "Human Capital and Growth: Theory and Evidence," *Carnegie-Rochester Conference Series on Public Policy*, 32: 251–86.

Sargent John F. Jr. and Dana A. Shea (2014). "The President's Office of Science and Technology Policy (OSTP): Issues for Congress," *Congressional Research Services Report 7-5700.

Schooley, James F. (2000). *Responding to National Needs: The National Bureau of Standards Becomes the National Institute of Standards and Technology, 1969–1993*, Washington, DC: U.S. National Institute of Standards and Technology.

Schultz, Theodore W. (1975). "The Value of the Ability to Deal with Disequilibria," *Journal of Economic Literature*, 13: 827–46.

Sink, Claire H. and Kevin Easley (1994). "The Basis for U.S. Department of Energy Technology Transfer in the 1990s," *Journal of Technology Transfer*, 19: 52–62.

Tassey, Gregory (2020). "Globalization and the High-Tech Policy Response," *Annals of Science and Technology Policy*, 4: 211–376.

Trump, President Donald (undated). *The President's Management Agenda*, https://www.whitehouse.gov/omb/management/pma/ (accessed February 3, 2020).

Westhead, Paul and Stephen Batstone (1998). "Independent Technology-Based Firms: The Perceived Benefits of a Science Park Location," *Urban Studies*, 35: 2197–2219.

Winston, Clifford (2006). *Government Failure versus Market Failure: Microeconomics Policy Research and Government Performance*, Washington, DC: American Enterprise Institute.

Wu, Kepi (1994). "A Partnership Approach to Successful, Cost-Effective Technology Transfer," *Journal of Technology Transfer*, 19: 4–12.

Index